31285

PN
4121   POWELL
.P58   Executive speaking;
            an acquired skill

EXECUTIVE SPEAKING
an acquired skill

Throughout history many people have tried to put the importance of speaking ability in historical perspective but no one has ever said it better than Bruce Barton.*

"IN MY LIBRARY ARE ABOUT A THOUSAND VOLUMES OF BIOGRAPHY—A ROUGH CALCULATION INDICATES THAT MORE OF THESE DEAL WITH MEN WHO HAVE TALKED THEMSELVES UPWARD THAN WITH ALL THE SCIENTISTS, WRITERS, SAINTS AND DOERS COMBINED. TALKERS HAVE ALWAYS RULED. THEY WILL CONTINUE TO RULE. THE SMART THING IS TO JOIN THEM."

*Bruce Barton (1886-1967) was a sales executive, businessman, scholar, editor, author, congressman and founder of the advertising agency: Batten, Barton, Durstine and Osborn.

EXECUTIVE SPEAKING
an acquired skill

by J. Lewis Powell

BNA Incorporated, Washington, D. C.

Printed in the United States of America
Library of Congress Catalog Card Number: 78–188829
ISBN 0–87179–176–5

Contents

Introduction

YOU CAN DO IT!

There are still many executives who are poor speakers. The significant fact is that most of them are at the upper echelons heading into retirement. They came up in a different era, under different conditions, when verbal communication had a lower priority among executive skills. Now and increasingly for the forseeable future, it appears that verbal confrontations, explanations, and presentations before city, state, county, and federal agencies and an endless array of community, citizen, and consumer groups will be a significant part of every executive's job.

It is significant that increasingly most of those moving up to replace senior executives are effective speakers. Technically competent but inarticulate executives are a vanishing species. They are being replaced by a new breed who not only have executive and professional competence, but can communicate effectively. Note the spectacular growth of the excellent Toastmasters Clubs. The young executive who wants to move up, but is not learning to communicate effectively, is limiting his career possibilities.

Obviously, young people who are not learning to speak effectively should expect their careers to level off short of upper-echelon management responsibility. Otherwise your organization will face this classic management dilemma—the person who has the necessary technical experience and background for promotion lacks the potential to grow into his new position. More particularly, he is not qualified to become an effective spokesman for his organization, a valuable voice for management in dealing with the public, the press, government agencies, consumer groups, congressional committees, etc. When an organization or an industry gets caught in the whirlwind of highly controversial news, there is little public sympathy for the viewpoint of the organization with inarticulate executives.

This is not a book about oratory, elocution, declamation, lecturing, debating, etc. Its emphasis and focus is on effective

1

speaking—the merchandising of good ideas through skilled verbal communication. It is a "how-to" book by a "can-do" speaker.

Today's traveler can go from New York to Moscow in less time than it took George Washington to go from New York to Philadelphia. Similarly, today's thinking man can go further and faster in his career than could the ambitious man of colonial days. Just as improved technology has speeded-up the path of progress for the traveler, improved techniques of personal communication can speed up the path of progress for the thinking man.

The fact that you are reading this book indicates:

1. *You are an uncommon person,* self reliant, and willing to invest some of your time in self-improvement. Therefore you are a member of a minority.

2. *You have potential.* Every man has more ability than he thinks he has; frequently, even more ability than the boss thinks he has. It is fact that most people perform at only a fraction of their potential.

3. *You recognize the need for continued learning.* An undeveloped talent is about as valuable as an unmined diamond.

Every man's progress toward his career goals depends not only on his talents but also on his ability to merchandise them. If you were an office boy, content to remain one, you would not have to worry about displaying your talent. Like a gold fish in an aquarium, the office boy's performance and potential are on display every working hour. However, if you want to keep moving, increasingly it will become necessary for you to find opportunities to display your potential.

This book is not for the mentally retarded, or the career dropouts, who believe they have gone about as far as they can go. This book is for the influential 5 percent who are making things happen now, and the up-coming 5 percent who will make even more important things happen in the future.

As you move up the career ladder in any field, you get paid less and less for personally doing things; but you also get paid more and more for your ability to motivate other people to do things. Therefore, increasingly your success will depend on your ability to communicate with other people. Your *ideas* can only be as valuable as your communication is effective.

Everything that man has ever accomplished, from the age of Adam to the age of the Atom, started with an "idea." Thought is the starting point of all accomplishment. But the ultimate value of every idea, including yours and mine, is completely dependent on our ability to communicate that idea. A person who has high-powered ideas but cannot communicate them is like an automobile with a high-powered engine but no transmission. He not only isn't going anywhere, he isn't even going to spin his wheels.

COMMUNICATION CREATES LEADERSHIP

The poorly communicated thoughts of a genius may have considerably less value than the well-communicated thoughts of a man of average intelligence. The ability to communicate either up-grades or down-grades the value of intelligence. You owe it to yourself to be able to speak and write as well as you think. Your communication must accurately project an image of your competence.

The greatest idea ever conceived may die at birth if the individual who conceived it lacks the ability to communicate it.

In an age of continuous confrontations, every effective executive must be able to merchandise ideas, concepts, policies, programs, proposals, and decisions, just as every effective salesman must be able to sell products and services.

Throughout history man has always had a surplus of spellbinding, almost hypnotic rabble rousers like Adolph Hitler. Even as in Samson's time, some people are still proving that the jawbone of an ass can be a deadly weapon.

Unfortunately throughout history mankind has also had a surplus of inarticulate, otherwise intelligent men, who exerted little or no influence. The ignoramus who is articulate may create little or big disasters, but the intelligent man who is inarticulate creates little or nothing.

When an audience lacks knowledge and expertise on a subject being discussed or debated, they tend to agree with the articulate speaker who speaks with confidence. It matters little whether he is right or wrong. The *law of mental acceptance is* that he who speaks with confidence creates conviction. Therefore, it is extremely important, to the well-being of the world, that the well-informed intelligent people learn to speak effectively so they will carry conviction.

Many an executive's opportunity for greater leadership, or for a major contribution to society, has been lost because he could not speak with the effectiveness necessary to create confidence.

One of the marks separating man from animals is his ability to communicate with the spoken word. Therefore, every intelligent man owes it to himself to acquire some skill in speaking. To an executive, speaking is a management tool just as is an adding machine to an accountant or a scalpel to a surgeon. Effective speaking is an acquired skill, and the executive who cannot speak effectively is one more unskilled person on the payroll.

SPEAKING AND LISTENING

There are many by-product skills that you will automatically acquire as an indirect result of becoming a more effective speaker. One of the most important of these skills is that you will listen more attentively. Did you ever attend an organizational conference where practically everyone involved is impatiently waiting for the man who has the floor to stop speaking so they can start speaking?

An instant replay would demonstrate few were listening.

Just as a good card player knows what cards have been played—a good speaker always listens and therefore knows what points have been made by the speakers who preceded him.

This alone will make you a man of distinction at most business conferences.

THE HANDICAPPED EXECUTIVE

When it comes to speaking in public most business executives suffer from three handicaps:

1. They have heard a tremendous number of distinguished men who were very undistinguished speakers. When it is their turn to speak they tend to imitate those they have heard.

2. Executives frequently have been exposed to the traditional high school or college course in "public speaking." As a result, they have unquestionably absorbed a lot of folklore about the importance of grammar, grooming and gestures. This trivia has little to do with effective communication.

3. Many executives naively believe that there are interesting and dull subjects, instead of realizing that it is the speaker who makes the subject interesting or dull. Just as the unenthusiastic workman alibis that he has an uninteresting job, the unenthusiastic speaker alibis that he has a dull subject.

Most organizations, when they refer to handicapped workers, mean *physically* handicapped employees. However, most of these workers are not handicapped in a way that interferes with their job performance. These so-called handicapped workers consistently set high standards of performance and production.

On the other hand, the handicapped executive who cannot speak effectively is unable to present his organization's viewpoint, whether to employees, the public, a union committee, or a senate hearing.

This executive's handicap limits his job performance and *should* interfere with his potential for promotion. Promoting an inarticulate man to the executive level is like hiring an engineer whose ability to use a slide rule can't hurt very much because he isn't very good at mathematics anyhow.

PUBLIC SPEAKING MYTHS

There are three self-defeating myths that keep many people from capitalizing on their ability to learn to speak effectively. When you no longer believe these myths you are well on your way to becoming an effective speaker, an effective communicator whose ideas will be of more value to yourself, your company and your community.

1. The oldest myth is that *speakers are born, not made.* For countless years this myth has served as a pre-fabricated alibi for the person who was either so uninformed that he believed it, or for the executive who had so much mental inertia that he did not want to be bothered acquiring the skills of his profession.

Recently, while enroute to Chicago's O'Hare Field, my seat companion and I were passing time discussing our respective business activities. He was a chemist who headed a department in his company. When he heard that I was a professional speaker who traveled a good deal staying at luxury hotels, speaking at conventions, business and professional meetings, he made the usual thoughtless remark: "**It must be wonderful to have a gift like that, to be a born speaker.**"

I replied somewhat cynically that it must be wonderful to have a gift like chemistry, to be a born chemist. He quickly corrected me and pointedly assured me that there was no such thing as a gift of chemistry, or a born chemist. You had to work at it, to learn it, he said. In some detail he described how his years of study and progressive, practical experience combined qualified him for his present professional status. He stated that if he had the *"gift"* of speaking he would have gone much further in the organization. He related how a man he hired as an assistant, fifteen years ago, was now the company's new president. In his words:

"In the beginning I had to teach him our business and even now he doesn't know more than I do about chemistry and our products, but he is a born speaker . . .

"Because he had the gift we let him represent the department, speak at meetings, and make presentations. As he learned our business he kept moving up because he had the gift of a being a speaker. Now he is president."

I was unable to convince my seat companion that maybe the new president had not only learned their business, but maybe somewhere along the way he had also used that same applied intelligence to acquire the executive skill of speaking effectively.

There are no born speakers any more than there are accountants born with adding machine skills. Effective speaking is an acquired skill. As in all other acquired skills, aptitude is generated by interest and attitude. The man who thinks he can— CAN!

2. The second myth is the belief that *speaking ability depends on the amount of schooling you have had.* Did you ever hear the alibi: "I can't speak effectively because I did not have much schooling?" Anyone who has ever attended a meeting of educators knows that speaking ability is unrelated to schooling. Almost everyone has sat through the ordeal of listening to a speaker who had more degrees than a dog has fleas, but who was an extremely poor speaker. Conversely, there are many exceptionally effective speakers who have had little formal schooling.

Spartacus is believed to have been an illiterate, yet he was one of the most effective speakers in history.

The relatively few good speaking courses in this country have produced thousands of effective speakers starting with people of all ages, from 17 to 77. Their graduates have included people with advanced degrees, and others who had not even completed grammar school. Many of their outstanding graduates started with pathetic self-consciousness, speech impediments, and even language handicaps. There is overwhelming evidence that no person of moderate intelligence can provide an acceptable alibi for not learning to better articulate his thinking.

On radio or TV "Amateur Hour" can be enjoyable to the audience and a great commercial for the sponsor, because each listener is equipped with a handy-dandy ON/OFF switch which works at his instant command. However, "'Amateur Hour" is not very enjoyable when you sit in an audience and watch an individual who is otherwise competent downgrade himself and his organization by his poor speaking performance. The executive or professional who haltingly mumbles his weary way through a poorly prepared talk at a meeting of intelligent people is broadcasting a bad commercial. Unfortunately, each listener at a meeting does not have an "ON/OFF" switch at his command. He will not remember what the speaker said—but he will long remember how poorly he said it.

3. The third myth is that *some executives are poor speakers because they are great thinkers.* The genius who thought up this fable was also able to convince his beautiful petite wife that the only reason he did not buy her a mink coat was that it would make her look short and fat. The truth is that it takes an organized mind to give an organized talk.

Speaking acts like a magnifying glass focused on the speaker. If he is competent, his competence will become more apparent. If he is incompetent, his incompetence will become more evident. In other words, when you are speaking to a knowledgeable audience the voice in action reflects the mind in motion.

WHAT THIS BOOK CAN DO

An effective presentation at a worthwhile meeting can produce these advantages to yourself and your organization:

(a) Favorable prestige and public acceptance that cannot be bought with paid advertising. For example, mention on the front page and coverage on prime time news broadcasts.

(b) Greater recognition and professional acceptance in your industry, your community, and your profession.

All these are available for the learning. Even if you are a victim of an old-time course in "public speaking," given by the English professor who couldn't speak, you can still overcome this handicap.

Learning to speak effectively is much easier than learning to be a parachute jumper—when learning to speak you don't have to succeed every time you try—you just have to keep trying.

This book won't help you become an old-time, spell-binding orator and it is equally unlikely to help you become even a new-age rabble rouser; but it will help you become a more effective communicator. If you are an exceptionally poor speaker, it will help you become a pretty good speaker; if you are a fair speaker, it will help you become a good speaker; and if you are already a good speaker, this book will help you become a better speaker. There is no speaker so good he can't become better. It is his decision.

Keep this book on your desk—refer to it often. Make it an important stepping stone in your career.

CHAPTER ONE

Choosing the Right Audience

Obviously, before you can speak it is necessary to have an audience. In the beginning, when your primary objective is to get experience, any non-objectionable, socially acceptable group having a routine meeting is a pretty good audience to learn your trade.

One of the best audiences at this stage in your speaking career would be a Toastmasters Club, preferably one not made up exclusively of people from your own organization, and very definitely not a club made up of people who work for you. People who work for you cannot candidly evaluate you. Unless they are fools or independently wealthy they usually applaud your speech and laugh at your jokes.

Many executives make the mistake of trying out their proposed speeches on their own subordinates. This is somewhat like reading an impartial history of the "War Between the States" written from the Confederate viewpoint. When an executive's subordinates tell him how wonderful his proposed talk is, he should treat this with the same healthy skepticism that a sick man would apply to a "Get-Well" card from the family undertaker.

A Toastmasters Club is designed to promote constructive criticism. Except for such clubs, it is almost impossible to get worthwhile criticism from strangers. Normally, at most meetings, when a speaker finishes, the chairman routinely tells the speaker how great he was and how valuable his contribution was. He proceeds through this ritual regardless of whether the speaker was good, bad or indifferent; it is part of the liturgy of meetings. Usually the chairman ceremoniously reads this flattery from notes that were written before he knew who was going to speak or about what. However, while the speaker usually should apply a generous discount to the chairman's remarks, he can with reasonable accuracy tell how good or bad he was by the reactions of the audience.

KNOW YOUR AUDIENCE

Before you accept any invitation to speak, and particularly when you are invited to speak at a meeting, it is most important that you get accurate information about the meeting— just as the people running the meeting insist on having background information about you. The bigger you are in your profession or organization, the more important this becomes.

In addition to routine information about the time, day, date, and place of the meeting, you also need to know the composition and approximate size of the audience, the subject on which they expect you to speak, the exact amount of time you will have, the purpose of the meeting, the nature of the occasion, and who else is on the program.

Without this information it is impossible for you to decide intelligently whether this is an appropriate audience for you or your organization, whether you should accept their invitation, or possibly recommend another speaker.

Having learned the importance of each of these questions the hard way, I finally developed a simple form which acts as a checklist so that I have the facts necessary for an intelligent decision (see speaker's checklist—Appendix III, page 125).

At least a couple of times a year when I ask for the "day and date" of the meeting, the day and date do not reconcile. Whether you mistakenly arrive a day early or late, it does not improve your image. Therefore, be sure of the day, date and time scheduled for your talk.

> In one case, by insisting on both city *and state,* I found out that although the man inviting me to speak was calling from Springfield, Illinois, the meeting was going to be in Springfield, Missouri! To some people Hot Springs means Virginia, but to others it means Arkansas.

There also should always be a clear understanding of who pays for what. Are you going to be reimbursed for expenses incurred, is there an honorarium involved, and is it clear that the organization having the meeting is providing all necessary props?

If you don't clarify these points, you won't be the first speaker who not only got billed for a suite of rooms that he did not need, but who also received a bill for cocktails ordered by other people and served in his suite both before and after the meeting. When he heard these things being ordered, he thought he and the others were enjoying the hospitality of the host organizations. The bills for the microphone or slide projector also may arrive at a later date.

If you are the wrong speaker on the wrong program and are lucky enough it may only involve a waste of time; more often the consequences will vary from an embarrassing situation to catastrophe that could cost you your job, and possibly permanently damage your career.

In our cartoon "Right Audience" we use a moderate example. We have an outstanding expert on "plant location" for industry address a group of ladies who thought they were going to be addressed by an expert on "plant location" for garden shrubs. Unfortunately for the speaker, the name of the organization was "Concerned Committee for Better Community Growth."

The names of organizations can be very deceptive. Frequently extremist groups and crackpots of all varieties have organizations whose names are purposely deceptive. By accepting an invitation to speak to such a group, your importance or that of your organization, may not only get them publicity, but it also may do a great deal of damage to your reputation and the prestige of your organization.

In order to attune your remarks to a specific audience you need to know the age groups involved. An example or anecdote which is meaningful to one age group may be meaningless to another. For example, when I speak at The Naval Academy, I have to keep reminding myself that I might as well use an example involving the Revolutionary War exploits of John Paul Jones as to use a World War II anecdote about Admiral Nimitz. (Both World War II and the American Revolution are ancient history to today's young people.)

On the other hand, if I were to address a mature audience of middle-aged executives who were adults at the time of World War II, references to Admiral Nimitz or General MacArthur would be very effective. To an audience under 50, mention of Lindberg's epic-making flight across the Atlantic is without much meaning.

For the same reason it is important to know the predominant levels of responsibility. You can put across the same message to an audience of production workers or top management executives, providing you do not use the identical words, anecdotes or examples.

> I learned the hard way that I should always ask detailed information about the composition of the audience. On one occasion I was extremely flattered to get an invitation to address a major meeting of "The Academy of Science" of an Eastern state. The letter of invitation emphasized that this would be their biggest and most important meeting of the year.
>
> Never did I prepare more diligently, and more stupidly, because I had failed to ask one seemingly irrelevant question. The night of the big event arrived. Backstage in a conference suite I could hear this great University's auditorium filling. One of the committee members rushed in to tell the committee chairman that attendance had just passed the 1,000 mark, making this by far the biggest meeting in the history of their organization.

When the time arrived I was escorted from the conference room to an off-stage position in the wings. Finally, with great pleasure, I listened to a very impressive introduction of myself. Bubbling over with immodest self-confidence, and exuding courage, I strode on stage prepared to deliver an impressive mind-stretching, thought-provoking, dignified address to the best scientific minds of the entire state. With impressive nonchalance I proceeded across the stage with downcast eyes, planning the dramatic impact of my brilliant opening. I reached the podium, turned dramatically and look up and faced that vast audience.

The impact was tremendous—not the impact on the audience but the impact on me! In front of me were 1,200 excited elementary school children who had competed in science fairs. Their average age was about 10 years. And my audience was not limited to the winners; it also included all the losers. (I had planned to open with comments on Dr. Kinsey's biological research!)

Everybody in the state knew about the traditional science fair meeting. However, I was from out of state and it had not occurred to me to ask if there would be children in the audience.

"What will be the composition of your audience?" is a vitally important question.

It is always valuable to know the purpose of a meeting. You may or may not want to participate in a political meeting; an explosively controversial meeting that's going to make news; or add your presence and the prestige of your organization to a special pressure group. No matter what decision you make it should be based on facts.

KNOW WHO'S WHO

Increasingly, it is becoming important to know what other speakers will be sharing the platform with you. Some years ago a prominent clergyman severely damaged his personal prestige by innocently accepting an invitation to speak at what appeared to be a non-controversial meeting. However, when the meeting got under way it developed that the program was loaded with extremists, promoting prejudice and bigotry. His presence guaranteed sensational publicity for both him and the meeting.

Even when you are told which other people have been *invited* to speak, always ask if they have accepted. Who has been invited to speak is not important, what matters is who has *agreed* to speak.

> Some years ago I encountered a program chairman who was a great con-man; as a result, his inconsequential organization has had a long and impressive list of prominent speakers. Having decided which prominent individuals he was going to snare, this chairman then wrote asking them to participate in a meeting and share the platform with an impressive list of prominent people who had also been invited. If his victim was an industrialist, the attached list of invited speakers read like a "who's who" of industry. Similarly, if his "chosen target" was a politician, the attached list was so politically important that the victim could hardly afford to say "NO". The only catch was that the letters of invitation did not go to most of the other people (who supposedly were going to share the platform).
>
> This technique was quite effective. Month after month he made the front page of the local newspaper, meeting one and sometimes two prominent people at the airport. He could honestly brag of having had an impressive list of prominent people as speakers.

KNOW YOUR SUBJECT

One of the most important questions that should be decided before you accept any speaking engagement is: were you invited as an individual or as a representative of your organization? Frequently this question isn't fully discussed until after your organization has made the headlines. If you want to get some fast notoriety, say something controversial. Although you're a minor executive you may read in the headlines: "Executive of (insert name of your company) criticizes President of the United States!"

Under no circumstances should you agree to speak on a subject that is not in your area of competence. Obviously you cannot speak with confidence and conviction on a subject about which you know little or nothing, unless you are an actor.

When you are asked to speak as a representative of your organization it is of particular importance that you agree to speak only on subjects that are within your area of responsibility. Otherwise recommend someone in your organization who is competent to speak on the subject. A seemingly innocent remark by a lower-level manager or professional, unfamiliar with the nuances of top management's position on a sensitive issue, can create a major crisis. Full-page ads are an awfully expensive way of correcting a public-relations boner.

In summary, before you can decide if you are the right speaker for an audience you need to know many facts. By knowing the questions to ask, you can intelligently decide whether any audience is the right audience for you or for your organization.

Requests for top executives as speakers should be thoroughly checked out. For example, when I was in the Pentagon we had an almost command request, from an important congressman, to send a prominent general to Cleveland to make the opening remarks at a veteran's meeting. At first glance it looked like an opportunity for worthwhile public relations. However, a little staff work, including a direct contact with the program chairman, revealed that although he definitely wanted that newsworthly general to be present he definitely did not want him to make any remarks. All he wanted was to have the general show up, in uniform, to add color to the occasion. As an afterthought, he indicated that maybe it would be a good idea to have the general lead the pledge of allegience to the flag! With the brusqueness of an ex G.I. he summed up his convictions by saying: "This is a military ball; we don't want any damn general speaking. We just want him to decorate the head table while we get on with the drinking and dancing."

* * *

In a slightly different situation when I was running interference for a prominent civilian executive, we received a request to have him speak at a large meeting of college women. Contacting the program chairman, we asked what she wanted the executive to talk about. Fortunately, she named a very specific subject. In response to further questions she steadfastly insisted that her members had a great interest in this particular subject. At this point we explained that she was very fortunate to have picked that subject because although our top executive was not familiar with that subject, we did have an articulate man on the staff who was a qualified expert, and we would send him to her meeting. Before slamming the phone her informative reply was: "A hell of a lot of publicity I would get from having that 'unknown so and so' on our program."

Every individual speaker should have criteria which enables him to accept only those engagements where he will be the right speaker to the right audience on the right occasion. This way he maximizes his opportunities for sustained success.

More importantly, any organization sophisticated enough to have a policy on advertising, public relations, or marketing should have also an established policy and a quality control governing who speaks for the organization, where, when, and under what circumstances. (Have you ever heard one of your own executives speak? Did he help or hurt your organization?)

When BNA filmed "Unaccustomed As They Are" in New York we were worried that Bob Milli, playing the role of Dave Garver, would over-do his satire of the young executive speaking at a business meeting. Our fears were groundless. Within ten days after the filming I attended three business meetings and heard and saw three executives make such poor presentations that they made the Dave Garver satire look good.

The following is a transcript of a young executive's opening remarks at a management seminar for mature, experienced, upper echelon senior executives in a specialized industry. Only the names of the persons, places and industry involved have been changed (to protect the guilty):

"Good morning—you are probably less surprised to see me than I am to see you. Up until Friday morning I never had heard about you, or this meeting! Friday morning I went to play a few holes of golf before work. (I am a member of the early birds.) John Smith said to me, 'How would you like to go to Happy Acres on Monday and give a talk to a bunch of production executives?'

I asked: 'What should I talk about?' John said it didn't make much difference since I was going to substitute for someone who wasn't going to show up anyway. Then I asked John what business you were in. When he told me, I reminded him that your industry was not my specialty, however he told me you were a bunch of nice guys and Happy Acres was a lovely place. So I said I'd go—and here I am, after all that's how we get business.

My specialty, aerospace, is pretty slack now—so I guess I better learn about other businesses. So I got a bunch of books and spent the weekend with them. Since these books are my brains I brought them with me. They are right here." He pointed to a three-foot stack of books.

After this overpowering opening, he gave an elementary talk about their specialized industry to its future presidents. He then came to the question period. Here he did a little better because most questions put to him were charitably related to his specialty and not to the subject of the meeting.

I am sure that he and his company will get a routine thank-you letter and neither he nor his employer will know what an excellent, long-lasting job he did of "unselling" a prestigious firm.

Paraphrasing a statement usually attributed to Charles Kettering: "Every so often a man should ask himself if he would be worth more to his organization if he stayed home."

As Peter Drucker points out in his excellent book "The Effective Executive" (page 52): "The effective executive focuses on contribution, he looks up from his work and outward towards goals. He asks: What can I contribute that will significantly affect the performance and the results of the institution I serve? His stress is on responsibility."

The above quote applies to the function of an executive as a speaker, just as it does to all other executive functions.

When considering an invitation to speak you should consider these dimensions of the decision:

What action will contribute the optimum benefit of:

(a) The organization which I represent,

and

(b) The success of this meeting?

In other words, as an effective executive you realize that neither you nor the audience should spend any time that does not produce proportionate results.

On the basis of these considerations you may logically decide to accept, reject, provide an outside professional speaker, or recommend someone else, either from within or outside your organization.

But unless an upper-echelon executive is still at the stage of desperately needing speaking practice, he would carefully consider how much of that scarce commodity "his executive time" should be spent speaking at each particular meeting. Frequently, what is really wanted is a speaker to represent the organization.

Many invitations are addressed to a specific upper-echelon executive merely as a courtesy. It is assumed that he will delegate the specific assignment to an appropriate person in whom he has confidence. Quoting once again from Peter Drucker's "The Effective Executive":

> "The chief executive mentioned above who had to dine out every night found, when he analyzed these dinners, that at least one third would proceed just as well without anyone from the company's senior management. In fact, he found (somewhat to his chagrin) that his acceptance of a good many of these invitations was by no means welcome to his hosts. They had invited him as a polite gesture. But they had fully expected to be turned down and did not quite know what to do with him when he accepted."

Frequently more good will, favorable publicity and customer respect can be generated by providing a top flight "outside" professional speaker for a meeting in which your company has a particular interest. Not only will this gesture create excellent goodwill for your organization, but it will also save a substantial amount of the high-priced time of both the key executive and his staff. It also keeps your top executive from being over-exposed.

CHAPTER TWO

Have Something Worth Saying

Just as every business meeting should have a definite purpose, every talk should have a definite message.

The message becomes the central theme, the backbone of your talk. Everything you say—serious or humorous—should be related to the theme of your talk.

As Will Rogers used to say everyone is ignorant about something. Always assume your audience is intelligent and ignorant. Because they are intelligent enough to know they are ignorant about something, they want you to better inform them on that subject. Ignorance is a prerequisite to learning— I have never met an intelligent man who did not know his own limitations.

But before you can determine and develop your theme, it is equally important to determine your purpose in speaking. What are your goals?

To tell the audience something they don't know?

Up-date the audience's existing knowledge?

Ask for action? Join-up?
Ask for contributions? Money?
Inform? Entertain? Educate?

You need to define your goals for two reasons:

1. You must orient your thinking and technique of presentation to its purpose, just as you orient it to your message.
2. Unless you have defined your objectives it is impossible to evaluate the degree of success obtained.

In the cartoon we use a historic message that has echoed and re-echoed down the corridors of time; and changed the destiny of nations. Patrick Henry's immortal—

"GIVE ME LIBERTY OR GIVE ME DEATH"

That was the theme, a message, that made a memorable impact. He could have said it a thousand other ways, for example, in the anguished fantasy language of a civil service job description:

> It shall be the direct, and indirect responsibility, of the colonial incumbent of this position of colonial residence, to obtain and implement direct access to the responsibility of making personal decisions in those areas of behavior (i.e. human behavior) where together with other colonial incumbents of similar and/or comparable colonial states, they may decide to establish and/or reestablish customs, habits and modes of economic, political and social behavior subject to such amendments, modifications as contra-indicated by a cessation of the bodily functions to the point of totality.

Similarly he could have fouled up the great idea by using the learned language of lawyers, the elongated erudite English of educators or the evasive English of a politician's promise. But he did not use any of these styles. Succinctly, with clarity, he summed up his message in seven words.

Pinpointing the specific message is the starting point of every good presentation. *The more concisely you can summarize your message the better your talk.*

To start preparing a talk before you have a message would be like going to an airline ticket office and saying: "I want to buy a ticket". Then when the clerk asked your destination you would reply: "I have not yet decided where I want to go, all I want to do is get going! When I am on my way I will decide on my destination."

It sounds stupid, yet many a talk has been prepared by a parallel procedure. Failure to use proper techniques in the right sequence is why it usually takes more time and effort to prepare a *poor* talk than would be required to prepare a *good* talk with proper techniques used in the right sequence.

If you don't use screwdrivers to drive nails, and hammers to fasten screws, why not become familiar with the right tools and techniques when preparing a talk? Start with a sharply defined message.

Sometimes this message comes in a flash, sometimes it is as difficult as trying to slash your throat with an electric razor. But unless you pinpoint your message, your indecision will be transmitted to your audience. If you are not sure what you are talking about, how can the audience be expected to know?

> Sometimes when I am trying to define a message I pretend it's the day after the meeting. A member of my audience can't find a football game on TV, so he is talking to his wife, who asks: "What did Joe Powell talk about?" If he cannot answer in one sentence—I goofed.

> Recently one evening when our television was broken, my wife and I were talking. She had just returned from a professional meeting so I asked her what the speaker had talked about. She replied: "He talked about forty minutes too long".

A different but related point is illustrated in the anecdote about the very laconic President Coolidge who never wasted a single word. One Sunday when Mrs. Coolidge was not feeling well he went to church by himself. When he returned, Mrs. Coolidge asked the President what the preacher had spoken about. His one-word reply was "SIN". Mrs. Coolidge then inquired what did the preacher say about sin—President Coolidge replied "I *THINK* he was against it."

Obviously your talk should not leave people guessing about what you meant. Your message should be attuned to the audience and pertinent to the occasion. It is not recommended that you speak about the natural superiority of Jewish scholars at the graduation ceremony of an Arab university.

Your message may or may not be the title of your talk, but the title of your talk, like an entry on a menu in a good restaurant, should be appetizing. Unfortunately, since most meeting programs are not as appetizing as most menus, meeting attendance suffers. After reading some deadly dull programs of meetings at which I was going to be a speaker, I have debated whether I would even attend to hear myself speak.

If many of the people who compose meeting programs opened restaurants they would delete from the menu such items as:

"Diamond Jim Brady—double cut rare succulent roast beef"

and replace it with the technically accurate: "Half-cooked thick slice of dead steer"

Sometimes a mentally intriguing title can be your message. Some examples would be:

"Automation—Friend or Foe"

"Learn to Live—with your computer"

"Profits in Perspective"

The title and the message should always fit like a hand in a glove. However, not every good message makes a good title, nor does every intriguing title make a good message.

Always start preparing your talk with a sharply defined message regardless of whether it makes a good title. Later you can decide on the title. Here are some examples of titles and messages that are not identical.

"There are no "if's"
"If is a Management NO NO"

For either of the above titles the message might be "Management is what you do with what you've got." The speaker could relate the title to the message by developing the idea that you cannot measure a man's management ability by guessing what he would do: "IF"

If he had more men

If he had more money

If he had more authority

"How Many Thermostats do you Have?"

is a good title—the message might be: "What turns you on, or off?"

"On-the-Job Retirement or Training"

The message might be: "If you do not have on-the-job training, you will have on-the-job retirement".

"Holidays New and Old"

The message might be: "Reducing the work week by holidays". The speaker could then review the reasons that justified the establishment of Thanksgiving, Labor Day, etc. On the basis of the reasons given for establishing Labor Day, he might now justify a new holiday such as "Welfare Day".

"When and What do you Feed Your Mind?"

The message—"Just as your body needs good food, so does your mind". The speaker could then develop the need for continuous education and talk about the programs available in the company or community.

"How Good is Good Enough?"

This could launch a job improvement program, the message would be—"There is always a better way—find it." The speaker could then develop the theme along these lines: any worker, or executive, who thinks his job is being done as well as it can be done obviously lacks both intelligence and imagination. With tongue in cheek the speaker might even propose a program of periodic salary decreases for people who don't propose job improvements.

The old Chinese proverb says every journey, long or short, starts with the first step. The first step in preparing a good talk, long or short, is to state a clear, concise message.

The more concise your message the less likely it is that the beginning and end of your talk will be too far apart.

CHAPTER THREE

Create and Capture Ideas

Ideas are more powerful than armies. You probably will never command an army; but if you can capture an idea and dramatize it, you may change the world.

A long time ago some homespun King Solomon made the sage observation: "The trouble with adult education is that to keep learning you have to keep unlearning what you learned as a child." Frequently unlearning what you were taught as a child can be difficult, about as difficult as unlearning how to ride a bicycle.

About half of what you were taught in school is of little value and the other half is priceless. The trouble is that neither you, I, nor your teacher has any valid idea which half is which.

I am told that people who can't swim frequently write books about swimming, and people who can't sell write books on selling. It also seems people who can't speak write books about speaking, and not being handicapped by experience, they repeat with equal conviction both the facts and folklore they learned in their research.

I hope that this book will not only cause you to learn, but also to *unlearn* a great deal of misinformation you have acquired about speaking.

Almost every book I have read about preparing a talk starts with the advice that the *first thing* you should do is prepare an outline. Frankly, I can't think of worse advice. Eventually a speaker should evolve an outline. But if he starts by preparing an outline, he will have created a prefabricated mental straightjacket. His talk will be as dull as a detailed explanation of a Pentagon organization chart.

The next thing he will probably do is tell his secretary not to schedule anything for Tuesday afternoon at 2 P.M.—that's when he is going to use that outline to dictate his talk.

He may be able to make an appointment with his secretary for Tuesday at 2 P.M., but I assure you he will not be able to make an appointment with an idea for Tuesday at 2 P.M. If there is one man on earth who is not going to have a worthwhile idea on Tuesday at 2 o'clock, it will be our hero. Ideas, particularly good ideas, are as independent as the wind. Like the wind, they never come by appointment. They arrive without warning at the darndest times, in the darndest places, including barrooms, bathrooms and even bedrooms.

The man who starts with an outline has imprisoned his mind before he even starts thinking. His premature outline, like a bikini bathing suit, will eliminate much of the need for imagination. Experience indicates that speakers who start with preconceived outlines usually suffer from an incestuous cross-sterilization of dull ideas.

To trigger your thinking always start without a preconceived outline or sequence of ideas—*GO CREATIVE!*

Good talks don't start with words, they start with good ideas. When you go creative you don't have to think up creative ideas; all you have to do is capture them. The world is full of ideas. It is always round-up time for the mentally alert.

In Napoleon Hill's book "The Master Key to Riches" (page 102) he relates how Dr. Russell Conwell developed the talk "Acres of Diamonds". He gave that talk more than four thousand times, it earned over six million dollars, and later became a best-selling book. Dr. Conwell used the money to found Temple University of Philadelphia. But what is more important is he got his basic idea from a chance conversation with a cemetery caretaker.

George Westinghouse got his great idea for the air brake, which revolutionized railroads, from an article in a Sunday school magazine. Neither Orville nor Wilbur Wright ever received a high school diploma, but they developed the basic principles of aerodynamics, invented the airplane and changed the world. Their basic idea was triggered by a toy.

Once you have a message, go hunting, capture every available fact, fantasy, folklore, or figure that even remotely relates to your message. At this stage all you want is quantity (quality comes later). Keep brainstorming your message, collect quips, historical facts, statistics, and even cartoons.

BE HONEST

If you elect to use a significant phrase or a significant portion of something previously said or written by some one else, be honest. Quote it and credit it to the person who said it. If you don't do this you may not only get involved in a law suit, you may also be exceedingly embarrassed if some one in the audience challenges you or if the knowledgeable press elects to comment on your indiscretion.

A few years ago a public official read a talk to a prestigeous audience at their annual convention in New York. The talk had been prepared by the official's staff who had very generously lifted many pages from a talk previously given by a professional speaker.

Somewhat to the surprise of the official, when he started reading these pages as his original thinking the audience first started tittering then some started walking out, no longer able to control their laughter.

Unfortunately, the official's speech writers apparently lacked competence as well as ethics. The material they had "lifted" was taken verbatim from the keynote address to this same convention, the previous year. The audience recognized the material.

IDEA CARDS

The way to capture ideas is simple. Just keep armed with blank 3x5 cards. I call them idea cards. Whenever and wherever you get an idea jot it down in the rough, one idea to one card. Forget about spelling or grammar. Just jot down every related raw idea; and capture it immediately, because ideas, like spring snow flakes on a mild day, disappear on contact. Under no circumstances try to concentrate or set aside a specific time.

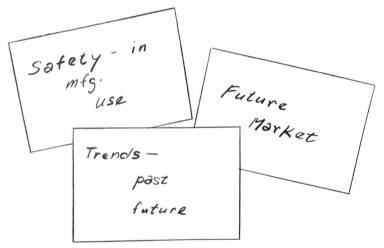

Capture your ideas, on the fly, in your odd moments. It is more impossible to be creative in an organized manner, than it is to say something funny on command. Keep your idea cards in your pocket, review them at every opportunity. You will not only discover that ideas breed much faster than rabbits, but you will also find yourself having great ideas on other subjects. These you can save for other purposes. Never forget one good idea, effectively communicated, can bring you fame and fortune.

Almost from the beginning of history man used the wind to turn a fan-like device he called a windmill. During much of this same time he used water power to rotate a variety of devices called water wheels. Yet it took thousands of years to think up the idea of reversing the process and using the fans and wheels to blow air and to propel boats. Both Fulton's steamboat and the mini-skirt came into being when man developed the idea that he no longer wanted to be dependent on the wind.

Every time you review your idea cards be curious. Speculate what would happen if you reversed the idea, magnified it or minimized it, etc.

Remember that your aim is primarily to seek ideas that are directly or indirectly related to the message of your talk. Actually, you will find that the fall-out from "Going Creative" will provide raw material for hundreds of talks on related subjects. You will have a reservoir overflowing with excellent material.

As you keep reviewing these ideas in your odd moments you will find yourself constantly refining, up-dating and improving them. You will literally have hundreds of ideas, a substantial number of which will be outstanding.

Assume you only had 9 ideas, like the 9 men on a baseball team, or like nine books on a shelf. Do you know how many different ways your 9 ideas could be arranged?

$$81 \quad ?$$
$$810 \quad ?$$
$$8010 \quad ?$$
$$10000 \quad ?$$
$$20000 \quad ?$$
$$50000 \quad ?$$
$$100,000 \quad ?$$

The answer is $9 \times 8 \times 7 \times 6 \times 5 \times 4 \times 3 \times 2 = ???, ???$

In other words, even as few as nine good ideas would provide you with hundreds of thousands of different treatments of your message.

CHAPTER FOUR

Get It All Together

Probably the two worst talks you will ever sit through are:

(a) the mumbling, methodical, monotone reader, even if his material is well-organized.

(b) the free-wheeling, loud and clear speaker who does not read, but whose material is completely disorganized. He is both confused and confusing.

To be effective you must have your material well organized. When you have guests for dinner it helps their digestion if you serve the food, from appetizer to dessert, in the appropriate sequence. When you are feeding the mind of an audience, it helps mental digestion if you serve your ideas in a similar sequence. Unorganized ideas frustrate an audience and create mental indigestion.

You have decided on your message, gone creative, and rounded up more ideas than you can use. Now it's time to get organized! You compound the effectiveness of your ideas by putting them in the particular sequence that will predispose the audience to accept them. The same ideas can be presented in a different sequence and predispose the audience to reject them.

For example, they tell a story about two seminarians who were studying for the priesthood. They got into a discussion as to whether it was all right to pray and smoke at the same time. To settle their differences, they decided to put the question separately to their superior. The next day, when they compared notes, they were amazed to find that they had received opposite answers to the same question. They then compared how they had worded the question. One had asked "Is it all right to smoke while I am praying?" He had received an emphatic "NO." The other had asked "When I am smoking is it all right to pray?" He was commended for his piety and assured that it was always desirable to pray at all times, no matter what one was doing.

Solitaire is the easiest way to organize your creative ideas— play solitaire with your accumulated idea cards:

1. Spread them out on a large surface so that you can see all of them at the same time.

2. Pick up and review each idea card individually. Place cards that deal with the same idea next to each other.

3. Combine concepts that are identical, or almost identical, by replacing them with a new card.

4. Start discriminating. Evaluate each idea card and discard any ideas that are not up to your standard of quality. Skim the cream and keep only the best ideas. Because you have an excess of quantity, you can afford to be selective. For example, no matter how mediocre a photographer you may be, the chances are that if you took 150 pictures and then picked the 10 best, those ten would be good.

5. Now you are working with the pick of the crop. These selected ideas are all thoroughbreds. Review them again. This time decide on the batting order—which idea should go first, last or in the middle. Play solitaire; move the cards to where you think each idea fits best in an effective

sequence. When you have put all the cards in sequence, review them again. Check the idea before and after each card for continuity of thought and make any indicated adjustments. You now have evolved an excellent outline of your talk—far superior to any outline you could have conceived in advance. A good outline is like good goulash—you don't make it, you accumulate it.

6. Now number the organized cards in sequence; but put a blank card after each four cards. Number the cards, including the blanks so you can pick them up and later put them down again in the same order, anywhere, anytime—at home, in the office, or in a hotel room, if you are a traveling man. The blank card is put in to serve as a reminder that you must continually clarify your ideas with "for instances," i.e., examples, illustrations, anecdotes, etc.

Now you have excellent ideas in the proper sequence, in contrast to the fellow who tried to dictate a talk and is now scraping the bottom of the barrel, desperately hunting for any ideas (even poor ones) because he has five pages to go. You have nothing but good ideas and probably more than you can use.

You are now ready to consider how you are going to best express these ideas—what words will dramatize your ideas so they will be enjoyed and remembered.

CHAPTER FIVE

Forget Your Textbook Grammar

You now have the message, the ideas, all the ingredients of a good talk. Like a chef with all the ingredients for a good meal, the question is how are you going to prepare and serve it? Which is the best way? There is no one best way equally good for all speakers. Because you are an individual you are unique— one of a kind. The words that are right for you could be wrong for somebody else and vice-versa. Did you ever listen to someone read a canned talk? It's about as exciting as an all-day rain at a picnic.

To make your talk interesting, do what comes naturally. Use your own words. Don't imitate anybody else; don't use a vocabulary, grammar, humor, or syntax that does not fit your personality anymore than you would wear another person's clothes that did not fit your body. Above all, don't worry about the petty details of academic English composition that you were taught 20 years ago.

Remember you are going to talk from notes. Since you are

not going to read your talk, your words can be altered both before and during your talk. You can weave your words to adjust to audience reaction as you go.

Steam pressure has almost limitless potential power, but it cannot motivate even a small electric motor, unless someone has acquired the skill to effectively convert that potential power into electricity. The only power on earth that can communicate with an electric motor is electricity. Similarly, the only power on earth that can communicate with people is language. Your ideas may have limitless potential but their real value depends on how effectively you can convert your ideas into words.

A good talk, like a good suit, should fit the wearer and at the same time it should be appropriate to the occasion. Just as a mature individual does not wear sports clothes to a formal dinner, or a tuxedo to a picnic, the mature speaker adjusts his words to both the audience and the occasion.

In one instance he may say: "We were told to expedite the transaction," while on another occasion he may say: "The boss said: 'get the lead out!' "

The information you originally obtained regarding the characteristics of your audience such as predominant age, occupations, education, income and levels of responsibility, provide you with an excellent frame of reference. (See Appendix III, p. 124.)

This advance audience profile clues you how to word your talk so it will be most meaningful and enjoyable to that particular audience. The same message can be delivered with equal effectiveness to a wide variety of audiences, providing you attune your words, examples and illustrations to each specific audience.

Words are the tools of the mind. Your ability to think is just as related to your vocabulary as the ability of a craftsman is related to the mechanical tools available to him. It is with words that we fashion ideas. We weave words into thoughts and use thoughts to crystallize concepts. The man of a limited vocabulary is necessarily a man of limited thinking ability, since he lacks the words with which to conceive ideas. For example, among many dialects on earth the word "stranger" does not exist; therefore, everyone necessarily has to be classified as either a friend or an enemy. Since the word stranger does not exist neither does the concept.

The relationship of words to concepts is like the relationship of the chicken to the egg. It's difficult to determine which comes first. As a person gains experience in speaking he develops not only a larger vocabulary, but also a sensitivity to the nuances of the words. He becomes aware of the difference between "liar" and "prevaricator," "error" and "mistake," "imply" and "infer." He stops misusing words as synonyms when they are not in fact synonyms. Consequently his thinking process improves.

Probably every adult is familiar with one of the many anecdotes that we use to illustrate the difference between the word "surprise" and "astonish." The story goes along these lines: The college English professor's wife arrived home unexpectedly and found the professor making ardent love to their maid. She screamed: "John! I am surprised!" He replied: "No my dear, you are astonished; I am the one who is surprised."

Words are to a speaker what instruments are to a surgeon. However, words not only transmit meaning but also trigger emotional reactions. For example, prohibition would never have been put into law if the proponents had merely talked about alcoholic beverages. When they substituted "demon rum" for "alcoholic beverage" they created a picturesque, unfavorable emotional reaction that carried more impact than a ton of logic.

Did you ever notice how your country has "intelligence agents" but the enemy has "spies?"

Similarly, I want my salesmen to be intensely dynamic but I regret that my competitor's salesmen are always too damned aggressive.

All of us consciously or unconsciously tilt words to create favorable or unfavorable impressions. For example when we are talking about a man who has had a number of jobs—

(a) If we like him—"he has had wide experience"
(b) If we don't like him "he was unable to keep a job"

Because words vary in their effectiveness in creating mental pictures and also vary in their emotional content, how you say something can be as important as what you say.

"How you say it" and "what you say" are heads and tails on the same coin. You cannot separate one from the other. To argue which is more important would be like arguing whether the length or the width of a square is more important.

WHAT YOU SAY × HOW YOU SAY IT = EFFECT

The more you improve both "what" and "how," the more you multiply the effectiveness of your communication. Conversely, if either "what" or "how" are weak, they will seriously damage your overall effectiveness.

Remember, $100 \times 0 = $ nothing
just as $0 \times 100 = $ nothing

Good causes are routinely damaged by poor choices of phraseology. Are you old enough to remember:

"What's good for . . . . is good for America?"

Suppose that gentleman had said: "What's good for America is good for . . . .?" The quotation would have meant exactly the same thing, except that the mental impact would have been psychologically positive instead of emotionally negative, and one corporation would not have become an exceptionally choice target for continuing criticism.

If you still doubt, "How you say it" is as important as "What you say," try a little experiment. The next time your wife returns from the beauty parlor with a new hair-do, say to her: *"Honey, you look like the first day after a long hard Winter."* When, and if, she ever starts speaking to you again, explain that your message was :"Honey you look as beautiful as the first day of Spring." But all you did was use an unfortunate choice of words.

Did you ever notice how people you like are ambitious, dynamic and determined, while those you dislike are greedy, aggressive and stubborn?

WORDS INTO CONCEPTS

Unless your audience is composed of people who move their lips when they read their comic books, they don't think in terms of individual words. They think in terms of phrases, ideas, concepts.

A speaker uses words to create concepts and phrases, to package ideas. He should not speak one word at a time any more than he would read a book one word at a time. Your ideas that will be remembered are the ones that create mental pictures. Audiences react to phrases not words. The speaker weaves words into packaged ideas.

For example, many thousand non-packaged individual words could not convey the mental impact of this packaged phraseology:

"Future historians will describe the age of the seventies as the one in which man stood up to his neck in pollution, while he fired hygienic rockets at the moon."

Or this explanation of the relationships of United States and Canada attributed to a Canadian Prime Minister:

"It is like a mouse and an elephant sharing the same bed; when the elephant rolls over the mouse better be damn quick."

The Chinese proverb states that one picture is worth a thousand words—this also applies to word pictures. When you speak you create mental images. Books have been written on the family problems that are created when a man retires. Yet no one has said it better or brighter than the housewife who summed it all with this picturesque explanation:

"Retirement means twice as much husband in the house and half as much income."

Avoid non-picturesque, boring language even though it is as grammatically correct as a school boy's English composition. As far as speaking is concerned, if it does not deliver the message with a mental impact that is remembered, "it ain't good grammar."

Since a good talk must always be related to the audience it is almost impossible to say "you" too often—such as *"You* will be affected"—"This will affect *your* family"—*"Your* interest is involved." Always personalize your message. Never let it be an abstraction. Talk about people, not about population. Even if you are talking about an abstraction like consumer, give it emotional life by saying *you* as a consumer.

WHAT DO YOU MEAN

Words mean different things in different places. For example, in Europe the term "Yankee" means any and all people from the United States. However, to any red-blooded Southerner Yankee is not only a dirty word, it is only one half of a colloquial reference to a person from North of the Mason-Dixon line. To a person from Pennsylvania, or New York, Yankee refers to a New Englander. To a New Englander, Yankee means a person from Vermont, while to a person from Vermont, Yankee means a down Easterner from Maine.

In the accounts of the early days of Christianity it is not unusual to read how someone was *"STONED."* This as a somewhat different meaning than when we now say: "Charley was stoned at our convention." Obviously we mean Charley was feeling no pain, while the early-day Christian probably felt considerable pain.

Have you ever considered the many and varied meanings of the word "FAST?"

He walked FAST

The drawer was stuck FAST

To reduce he went on a thirty-day FAST

She was a FAST woman

He pulled a FAST one

The child was FAST asleep

They were FAST friends

Among words in the English language "FAST" is not unique in its variety of meanings. However, it is unique in that it provides a vivid example of how individual words depend on context for their meaning.

This is why a speaker should learn to speak in phrases and think in terms of concepts.

In much of the United States "kids" is a socially acceptable synonym for children. Some communities even have signs "Drive Slow We Love Our Kids." Yet in parts of the deep South "kids" is definitely uncouth and not socially acceptable.

In one part of the country "broad" is a good natured colloquial reference to an attractive young lady. However, in other parts of the country, unfortunately, it is a synonym for "street walker."

At one time when a parent boasted that his son was a four-letter man he meant his son was an athlete. Now he probably means his son is the editor of the college newspaper or possibly a popular playwright.

No businessman, if he wants to stay in business, can afford to forget that what he refers to as "Our most important *customer*"; is the same organization that his competitor refers to as "Our most important *prospect.*"

Did you ever notice that when an animal is in the field it may be referred to as a steer or a sheep, but when it is served cooked, sliced and on the table it is called beef or lamb.

The product which a salesman describes "as lightweight and inexpensive" is frequently described by the customer as "cheap and flimsy."

Since the end of World War II and the defeat of Adolph Hitler most people recognize that it is stupid to be anti-Semitic. However a great many people handicap themselves and limit their potential for greatness by being "anti-semantic."

Few people in this world can do as much good as a sincere, well-informed, enthusiastic, articulate person—however the reverse is also true, few people can do as much harm as:

The misinformed, enthusiastic, articulate person
or
The well-informed, sincere, inarticulate person.

Words are the instruments of the skilled brain, words are the greatest tools ever conceived by the mind of man. Learn to respect them, use them and enjoy them. The person who lacks words necessarily lacks ability.

Just as a gentleman never insults anyone by accident, a speaker should never use an emotionally charged word or a thoughtless word by accident. Don't be like the funeral director who thanked the grieving family for their prompt payment of his bill, adding: "I hope I will soon again have the pleasure of serving you."

WATCH YOUR LANGUAGE

Most English and/or American-speaking people fail to realize that there are two major and many minor dialects in their language—and that "never the twain shall meet." All of us switch from one dialect to the other as the occasion demands. These two dialects are:

SPOKEN ENGLISH
and
WRITTEN ENGLISH

They use different syntax, grammar, vocabulary and sentence structure. Generally speaking, what is good style in one dialect is poor style in the other. For example, if you had an exact verbatim transcript of a brilliant talk it would make miserable reading. Similarly, if an alleged speaker reads verbatim an excellent piece of writing, it will make miserable listening.

An elementary example of spoken and written English is illustrated by the salutation we use when we meet someone in person as compared to the salutation we use when we write a letter:

Spoken—"Hi Joe" or "Hello Joe."
Written—"Dear Joe"

The printed menu says: "succulent salisbury steak"; but we tell the waitress "I'll take the hamburger."

Effective spoken communication uses short words, short direct sentences—plus such subtle nuances as inflection, pauses, change of pace, and changes of tone. The poor acoustics of many meeting rooms distort long words.

Effective written communication uses longer words, longer sentences, including indirect sentences, printed punctuation, commas, semi-colons and mechanics such as parentheses, etc.

A listener must listen at whatever speed the speaker speaks; but a reader sub-consciously adjusts his speed of reading to the complexity of the material, etc. If the reader doesn't grasp a meaning on the first bounce he merely backs up and re-reads. A member of your audience cannot back up and re-listen.

Within the spoken and written dialects of English there are many colloquialisms and jargons such as legal language, academic English, business English, and government English. None of this jargon should be used unless your audience is composed exclusively of people who speak that particular jargon. The word "security" does not mean the same thing to a banker, military officer and a safety engineer. And the word housebreaking has a different meaning to a policeman and the owner of a puppy.

Initials and coined anagrams, in particular, can be very deceptive. Therefore you should either avoid them entirely or spell out what they mean.

S.O.B. has a uniform meaning throughout most of the English-speaking world, but in Washington, D. C. it means Senate Office Building.

It is not equally well known that A.B.A. and A.M.A. have a variety of meanings to different people, for example:

A.B.A.   American Bankers Association
           American Bar Association
           American Basketball Association

A.M.A.   American Medical Association
           American Management Association
           American Motel Association

One time I attended a Pentagon briefing given by a senior military officer. Throughout his prepared presentation he repeatedly used the word "MAP'S." It was twenty-four hours later that I found out everytime he said "MAP'S' he meant "Military Assistance Programs." I am sure some people never found out what he meant.

DRAMATIC WORDS AND PHRASES

In speaking, there are many techniques of using words that can dramatize your ideas so that they will be remembered.

Rhythm

One such method is to use a phrase with rhythm, such as:
"Burn Baby Burn"
"Fifty-Four Forty or Fight"

Both of the above were not only remembered—they changed history.

Twists

Another extremely effective method is to twist a well-known expression such as:

"The butcher, the baker, the candle stick maker."

In Detroit they say:

"The butcher, the baker, the Cadillac maker."

Or remember the phrase:

"Came in like a lion and went out like a lamb."

Under appropriate alcoholic circumstances this could be changed to:

"He came in like a lion, and went out like a lamp."

Or did you ever hear:

"A garden is a thing of beauty and a JOB forever."

or

"A shotgun wedding is frequently a matter of wife or death."

For some reason, unknown to me, phrases using alliteration are always mentally digestible, emotionally satisfying, and easily remembered; for example:

"Senior Citizen"
"Poverty Program"
"Sex and the Single Girl"

Figurative expressions

These may also involve rhythm or alliteration but the important thing is that they create pictures.

Pork Barrel
Bureaucratic Bumbling
Brain Washed
Iron Curtain
Boob Tube
Arsenal of Democracy

Slogans

These are catch phrases like:

Safety First
Remember the Maine
New Deal
Tiger in Your Tank

SIMILES

There is no better way to make your point crystal clear and cause it to be remembered than to illustrate your point with a simile that is either homespun, picturesque, humorous, whimsical, or incongruous. The words "like" and "as" are invaluable, such as:

"It was a pleasant and unexpected surprise *like* discovering the reason your check book didn't balance was because you had forgotten to post a deposit."

*   *   *

When an old man marries a young woman it is *like* an illiterate buying a book for someone else to read.

*   *   *

Doing business without advertising is *like* winking at a girl in the dark, you know what you want to do but nobody else does, including the girl.

*   *   *

He was as welcome a visitor *as* a nervous polecat at a picnic.

*   *   *

This approach proved difficult, it was *like* trying to play tennis by yourself.

*   *   *

No one is always wrong, most of us *like* stopped clocks are right about twice a day.

*   *   *

Public officials enjoy about as much privacy *as* statues in the park.

*   *   *

Government regulation of our industry is *as* unnecessary as a fence around the cemetery—those inside are too involved to get out and those outside don't want to get in.

*   *   *

He was as unimaginative, and as handicapped, *as* a politician without a promise.

*   *   *

It was as frustrating *as* arguing with a computer.

*   *   *

It was impossible, *like* trying to resign from a book club.

*   *   *

Like throwing out the baby with the dirty bath water.

*   *   *

It depends on how you look at it. Its *like* looking at a quart bottle of liquor with one pint gone. Is it half empty or half full?

*   *   *

Computers are *like* women, it is difficult to live with them or without them.

*   *   *

Alimony is *like* buying hay for a horse that has been stolen.

*   *   *

Its a sporting proposition *like* telling time by an automobile clock.

*   *   *

Its easy *like* being charitable with another persons money.

*   *   *

Like employing a fox to be watchdog in the hen house.

*   *   *

Reverse logic and double negatives can make similes that are particularly intriguing such as:

It is difficult to win a debate when your opponent is not handicapped by a knowledge of the facts.

*   *   *

About *as* permanent *as* a permanent wave.

*   *   *

It was absurdly simple *like* the new simplified income tax form—more absurd than simple.

*   *   *

Poor salesmen are *like* bachelors, they won't take yes for an answer.

*   *   *

It is an unusual procedure *like* a motorcycle policeman using training wheels.

*   *   *

Probably the greatest example of how similes can combine wit, wisdom and information is this classic:

A bachelor's report on a weekend visit.

If the soup has been *as* warm *as* the wine, and the wine *as* old *as* the chicken, and the chicken *as* tender *as* the maid, and the maid *as* willing *as* the duchess I would have had a wonderful time. (Reader's Digest p. 119 March '56)

PHRASES

Effective speaking is achieved when you can translate good ideas into active words that create mental pictures in the minds of the listeners. Examine every point you are going to make. Reinforce it with some "for examples," "for instances," "in other words," and whenever appropriate, illustrate it with vividly picturesque word descriptions. For example, President Kennedy, speaking about an economic upturn:

"The incoming tide raises all the ships in the harbor."

Or the European economist talking about how his country's economic prosperity was related to the fluctuating uncertain value of the U. S. dollar:

"It's like shooting white water rapids in a canoe with a nervous elephant for a companion."

Once you have made your point with logic, don't hestitate to reinforce it with quotable quotes. Dramatize it with examples, illustrations, figures of speech, word pictures. Winston Churchill describing Russia as:

"A riddle, wrapped in a mystery, inside an enigma."

Or consider the vivid clarity created by the use of almost homespun words, blended with the skillful repetition of the three one-syllable words "has made us," in President Kennedy's speech to the Canadian Parliament:

"Geography *has made us* neighbors.

History *has made us* friends.

Economics *has made us* partners.

Necessity *has made us* allies."

These phrases are not only remembered, they frequently make news, thus:

Vast T.V. Wasteland

Politics is the art of getting money from the rich and votes from the poor.

Failure is the path of least persistence.

All blood has the same color.

Nobody bats a thousand; even teenagers are not always infallible.

Experience should be used as a springboard, not as a parking meter.

Never resent growing old; not everyone gets the opportunity.

Speaking is like sex; depending on your skill and attitude, you may merely meet an obligation or enjoy a shared sensation.

PRACTICE THE WORDING

Once you start converting your ideas into words, keep talking about your ideas at every opportunity to anybody who will listen. At home, at the office, at the club. etc. Without effort you will develop a skill with words, an enthusiasm for your subject, and find you have the ability to coin a phrase or create an up-dated cliche. As a result, you will be much more at ease when you give your talk.

Since you are going to talk your talk, your only need for writing is a mental exercise to be sure that you have continuity and timing. Remember, the recipe for a good talk always includes plenty of shortening.

CHAPTER SIX

Create Interest With Fun, Facts and Figures

Humor is as essential to a talk as seasoning is to a good meal. Just as a skilled chef blends the kind and amount of seasoning to the kind of food he is preparing, an effective speaker relates the kind and amount of humor he uses to the kind of a talk he is preparing. In turn, the kind of talk he is preparing is governed by his audience and the nature of the occasion. Humor should come naturally—it should never be forced.

Do not confuse humor with jokes; leave jokes to professional comedians. Jokes are a specialty. They involve considerable talent and timing on the part of the comedian who tells them. But they do not *necessarily* involve a lot of intelligence on the part of either the speaker or the audience.

The type of humor a business executive or professional should use does not depend as much on timing as it does on the interplay of intelligence between the speaker and the audience. Everyone has some sense of humor; but not everyone has a sense of comedy. Unfortunately many occasional speakers keep trying to be stand-up comedians. People who are not comedians when they are sitting down seldom become comedians when they stand up to speak.

Unless you have the talent and timing of an undiscovered Bob Hope, forget about jokes. The only exception is a joke on yourself. Telling it will make you look human and the audience will identify with you, particularly if the joke on yourself involves an embarrassing moment.

Everything you say, either serious or humorous, should relate to your message, illustrate it, or dramatize your point. Never interrupt your audience's train of thought with unrelated humor. Using humor that is unrelated to your message is as appropriate as offering a drowning man a drink of water.

Also, never use any humor from the current issue of a popular magazine—the audience probably knows the story better than you do. On one sad occasion I heard four successive speakers open with the identical story; all had lifted it from the current issue of the Reader's Digest. The audience reaction varied from annoyance to disgust.

The humor an executive should use is that which involves intelligence, plays on words, incongruities, contrasts, illustrative anecdotes etc. In other words, the same type of humor that he uses in his day-to-day contacts. Humor that comes naturally is associated with intelligence. Every great man is known for his wit as well as for his wisdom. Books have been written about the wit of presidents, popes, statesmen, scientists, and scholars. The book has yet to be written about the jokes any great man told, but informed people still intellectually enjoy the humor of Churchill, Roosevelt, Pope John, Ben Franklin, and Einstein.

A professional comedian can tell an endless variety of unrelated jokes without continuity, each joke being a separate entity. But the humor a speaker uses must *always* be related to what precedes and what follows it. In other words, the speaker's humor should always have continuity, be relevant to the message and related to the audience. Unlike a joke it is not funny by itself; it is entertaining only because it is humorous in that situation, under these circumstances. What is funny in Peoria may or may not be funny in Pittsburgh. Humor involves an interplay between the audience's frame of reference and the intelligence of all involved.

> For example, at a company meeting in Omaha a breakfast was scheduled for the morning following a banquet and late night festivities. Unfortunately, some time during the night the hotel's hot water system broke down. Came the dawn, the survivors of the previous night's alcoholic festivities dragged themselves out of bed, prepared to shave and shower in order to simulate sobriety for the command attendance at the President's breakfast meeting. Then they discovered there was no hot water for showering or shaving, and when they went to breakfast they also discovered there would be neither coffee, tea, or any other beverage that required hot water.
>
> The first speaker faced a difficult disgruntled audience; their only frame of reference was hangovers and no hot water. Capitalizing on this the speaker opened with:
>
> "Despite last night's festivities, this is one meeting at which not a single person got into HOT WATER."
>
> The audience's pent-up emotional frustration converted to explosive laughter, everyone laughing at himself and at the situation.
>
> *   *   *
>
> I saw a so-called humorist fall flat at a convention in French Lick, Indiana. He had one hundred good anecdotes all related to Indiana, is geography, traditions, peculiarities, and people. Unfortunately, it was a national meeting and no one in the audience was from Indiana. Therefore, they had no pertinent frame of reference. Nothing the speaker said was humorous to that audience. However, at a state convention of people from Indiana his remarks would have been sensational.

While speaking of teenage marriages, a speaker dramatized his point by facetiously remarking that some of the kids in his community were so young when they married that they wrote letters to Santa Claus asking for a honeymoon trip to Disneyland.

Similarly, speaking after an expensive steak dinner, an executive quipped: "When you stop to consider what we paid for that steak it is no wonder cows are considered sacred in India."

Incongruous relevant statements can be particularly humorous. A speaker expressing his regret for a late arrival explained: "I will regret this incident to my dying day, if I live that long!"

Speaking at a planned parenthood meeting, a speaker intrigued the audience with this bit of whimsy: "Most people don't realize that having children is hereditary. If your parents did not have any children, it is unlikely you will have any."

There is nothing wrong with using a familiar anecdote as long as:

1. it illustrates your point
2. If you disarm the audience by reminding them that it is a familiar story.

For example, it is doubtful if anyone has developed a better illustration for:

Mixed Emotions: The feeling a man gets when he learns his mother-in-law drove off a cliff in his new Cadillac.

Satisfaction: The feeling you have when something doesn't wear out until you have completed the payments.

Dilemma: The problem the middle aged fisherman had when he caught the mermaid—on the one hand he had too much fish to love, on the other hand he had too much woman to eat.

If your talk is related to communism you can always illustrate the illusionary thinking of communism by pointing out that everyone had probably heard that Adam and Eve were Russian: "After all they had no clothes and little shelter, and even though they did not know where their next meal was coming from, they thought they were living in a workers' paradise."

Facetious definitions always provide humor such as "Advertising is the art of making people think they want something they never had." Some other examples:

A Career Girl: A girl who doesn't plan to marry until she is thirty and remains 29 until she marries.

Chemical Warfare: The eternal battle between blondes and brunettes.

Shooting dice is always a shaky business.

A good businessman is like a duck—he is calm on the surface, but underneath he paddles like hell.

Every occupation, every profession, every region, and every age has humor particularly pertinent to it. Similarly many situations create the opportunity to personalize your humor.

A final word about humor: don't misuse it. Legally a speaker may have the right to be vulgar, just as he has a right to pick his teeth, eat with his knife, or scratch his stomach in public. However, if he has any manners he will not do these things (particularly when he is at the head table.) Therefore, unless the speaker wants to cheapen the public's image of himself and downgrade his organization he should never include a vulgar joke, an off-color anecdote or a smutty story in his remarks. No matter how loud the audience laughs, *at that moment,* later some will say "I thought he was a bigger man" or "I used to think (insert name of your company) had class."

Vulgarity always detracts from the image of leadership. It is significant that even vulgar people don't want vulgar leaders.

When you prepare a talk you will never have to worry about whether there will be any ladies in the audience, IF YOU ALWAYS ASSUME THERE WILL BE GENTLEMEN IN THE AUDIENCE.

SOURCES OF FASCINATING FACTS

Unfortunately, during the process of growing up most of us are exposed to some very dull academic courses and forced to read dull school texts which allegedly dealt with history. Most of the material to which we were subjected was usually a sanitized and sterilized version of either military or economic history, tilted to suit the local authorities. Unfortunately, usually we were not told that this material was not necessarily the whole truth, nor were we warned that it usually only dealt with relatively specialized aspects of man's total history. Most often it dealt primarily with man's battles, wars, and the palace politics of transient political powers. It ignored most of man's inventions and epoch-making events which have determined the long-range history of mankind. For example, the invention of the moveable type printing press made possible the practical economic reproduction and stockpiling of knowledge, which made possible the education of the masses, self-education, and mass communication. It made practical the mass distribution of knowledge, facts, and events that stretched the minds of millions. It changed the world more than all the battles and wars that were ever fought. Yet few people know when, where, or how the moveable type printing press was invented.

You cannot have twentieth century civilization without machine tools; yet most people don't know what a machine tool is—or why they can't live without it, or how it creates leisure for the masses and makes culture available to millions.

Based on considerable reading and research, I doubt if there is a single industry, occupation or profession that does not have a colorful and fascinating history. These accounts sparkle with the amazing activities of sinners, scientists and saints. Motivated morons, rollicking rogues, benefactors, geniuses, professors, plodders and pushovers all make up the colorful cast of characters that created the age in which we now live. Their escapades and exploits include grave-robbing by medical students, weird, wonderful and hilarious inventions; experiments such as the character who concealed a horse inside an early locomotive to make the locomotive go faster, eternal pills that were recovered and used again, again and again by the same and/or different people.

Facts, anecdotes, and legends abound in the glamorous non-military history of man. Possibly because so many businessmen, scientists, engineers and professional people go around reading dull papers to audiences, we have created a myth that these fields don't have glamour, excitement and adventure. Much of this history is more thrilling and more fascinating than most mystery stories. Did you ever hear of Rumford's Baking Powder? It was named after Count Rumford (Benjamin Thompson) who was a fabulous flamboyant character who achieved distinction in many fields including being a spy, scientist, military officer, soldier of fortune, inventor, researcher, nutritionist, developer of the science of thermodynamics, promoter, scholar, inventor of the cooking stove, pioneer in ballistics, ladies' man, public benefactor, man about town, inventor of drip coffee and steam heat. He also proposed the founding of the American Military Academy at West Point and almost became its first commandant. Why he failed to become its commandant makes an even better story.

There is a gold mine of fascinating material in the history of occupations, industries and professions. Sometimes it's hilarious, as when Samuel Colt raised industrial capital by traveling with circus sideshows, intoxicating volunteers with laughing gas. Apparently by accident, he discovered complete anesthesia before the doctors but unfortunately did not recognize its value. From the standpoint of raising capital to patent his revolver—total anesthesia was almost an economic disaster.

These accounts, both hilarious and mind-stretching, are always filled with fascinating, relevant available illustrations that will make your talks far more interesting. No matter what field you are in, it has a colorful history.

Did you ever hear a speaker on insurance tell how Daniel Defoe, the creator of Robinson Crusoe, proposed a plan of insurance and social security that was 100 years ahead of its time?

Ask your insurance man about the "Tontine Craze" which was part of the gambling-era growing pains of the now sedate insurance industry. The "Tontine" really involved gambling on your life expectancy. As each subscriber died his annuity went to the survivors of the original group, the last survivor was the winner, and the winner took all. As the number of survivors got smaller and smaller so presumably did their chances of dying a natural death.

Did you ever hear a speaker enliven his talk with an account of how the occupation of barbering evolved into surgery, the profession to whom so many of us owe our continuing health and life?

To illustrate the wealth of reference material available, Appendix V (page 133) contains a list of such books on a variety of subjects. Each of these books in turn will make reference to many other interesting books dealing with equally fascinating aspects of these industries, occupations and professions.

HOW TO HANDLE CONTROVERSY

Sometimes you may antagonize an audience without realizing it by seeming to say: "This is so because I say so, and anybody who disagrees with me is stupid!"

When you present a controversial point of view, subject to debate, always offer proof, cite supporting evidence, give examples, refer to others who agree.

Since you are no longer a teen-ager you can't afford to act as if you believe yourself to be infallible. *Don't create controversy and invite rebuttal by your manner of presentation.* After all, you are trying to sell an idea, not to win a debate.

STATISTICS

Statistics in a speech have been described as being like lumps in mashed potatoes—the fewer the better. Similarily, it has been said that half the statistics in the world are invaluable and the other half are worthless. The trouble is nobody knows which half is which.

Statistics properly presented can be interesting, even exciting. Ask any red-blooded girl-watcher if he can get excited about statistics like 36-24-36 when they are properly presented in round figures.

For statistics to be interesting they must be meaningful in a frame of reference with which the audience is familiar on the basis of their own personal knowledge and experience. For example if a speaker says that a country has a population density of 700 people per square mile, only the people in the audience who are familiar with population density statistics know the significance of the "700" figure. Is it big or little?—more than Rhode Island? or less than India? However if the speaker had said:

"The population density statistics of Japan and of the United States make an interesting comparison."

(He would have aroused interest and prepared his audience for the following conclusion.)

"The population density of Japan is 700 persons per square mile as compared to 54 per square mile in the United States. In other words Japan is 13 times more densely populated than the United States."

This would have made the density per square mile statistics meaningful and relevant to his audience. A good rule to remember is to always relate the unfamiliar to the familiar. For example if you are speaking to an audience from Missouri, you could say Japan has an area of 142,000 square miles but it would be more meaningful if you said Japan has an area about twice as big as Missouri.

One way to make statistics interesting is to translate them into picture comparisons such as: if you had a stack of dollar bills 100 feet higher than the Washington Monument you

would have approximately $1,000,000 dollars; or if ever since the time of the Roman Emperor Claudius you had spent $200 a minute you still would not have spent as much as the proposed federal budget for next year. (See Appendix VI, p. 138.)

Always convert statistics to pictorial illustrations. Abstract numbers have little meaning to most ,people. For example: almost everyone knows that Alaska is the largest state in the union and Rhode Island the smallest, but did you know that Alaska is more than twice as big as Texas and more than 480 times as big as Rhode Island?

Statistics can be made understandable, and even fascinating, if you either maximize or minimize them so they relate to your listeners' frame of reference. For example, a breakdown of the exact figures on the composition of the world population expressed in millions and billions would be meaningless to most people. Yet it becomes quite interesting and understandable if you minimize it this way:

Suppose there were only 1,000 people in the world but they were divided into the same ratios as today's billions. The world of 1,000 would look something like this—

> 565 Asians
> 210 Europeans
> 140 North and South Americans
> 85 Africans

About 500 of these people would not be able to read or write, and 370 would live under communist domination. About 60 of these people would live in the U.S. They would have a life expectancy of 70 years while the remaining 940 would have an average life expectancy of 40 years.

To indicate that a ship is 1,000 feet long is not nearly as descriptive as saying it is about the length of three football gridirons. If you say the Houston Astrodome is 210 feet high it is a relatively meaningless abstraction, but if you say you could put a twenty-story building under its roof you create a meaningful picture.

Unless you are an accountant talking to other accountants, avoid "percentages." Most people instinctively think in common fractions—up to and including fifths—particularly people with scotch in their blood. You can say 66 percent of the earth's population go to bed hungry every night; but it becomes more understandable if you say two-thirds of the world's people go to bed hungry every night, or—even more meaningful— two out of every three people on earth go to bed hungry every night.

You can say 75 percent of the world's population is under 25 years of age, but it is more effective to say 3 out of every 4 people on earth are under 25. "Percentages" and "population" are abstractions while people and numbers are readily pictured.

When the figures are very large, hundreds of thousands, millions, billions, etc., if at all possible use the nearest approximate round number. Supplement it by using ½'s and ¼'s if absolutely necessary. Avoid expressions like 2.26 billion— instead say approximately 2¼ billion. Even then most people won't know what a billion is. When necessary you can always have exact figures available on a hand-out sheet, but no one can follow a speaker using involved figures. When using approximations understate rather than overstate. Then in case of controversy the precise figures will always strengthen your case.

Another absurdity is the speaker who quotes obvious gross estimates in precise numbers down to the last imprecise digit, such as:

"In 1969 the gross public debt of the United States was $353,720,253,841."

The truth of the matter is that no one could even prove that figure to the nearest million dollars so the remaining figure of 253,841 is a meaningless accounting fantasy, as impressive and as useful as ice skates in the Sahara.

> Following the recent California shift in real estate, which the rest of the country called an earthquake—I listened to two speakers on the subject. Both talked to the same audience about the same subject based on the same facts. One bored and confused the audience with his continued reference to numerical recordings on the Richter Scale which he used as his frame of reference. Most people knew, or subsequently guessed, that the Richter Scale was a method of measuring earthquake intensity. However none of us knew the significance of the

numbers quoted, whether they were "high" or "low" and how they compared to other recent earthquakes. He might as well have been speaking Latin or quoting stock market quotations in Roman numerals.

However the second speaker, who may have had less knowledge, made the same subject intensely interesting and more informative because he avoided getting involved in the technical details of the Richter Scale, yet at the same time he made reference to the Richter Scale meaningful. He put it in perspective by telling us initially what was a high and low rating, and then illustrating it with references to other earthquakes such as—the Alaska Good Friday earthquake of March 1964. From then he minimized references to the Richter Scale and talked in terms of our knowledge and experience, number of tremors, duration, property damage, etc.

Just as you avoid the jargon of your occupation—also avoid statistics and measurements that are unfamiliar to your audience.

MENTAL ARITHMETIC

Did you ever listen to one of these psuedo sophisticated speakers who expects his audience to do mental arithmetic— and ends up giving them instant mental arthritis. It usually goes like this:

"Last year the figure was 1,643,247,322.

This year it is 1,867,863,788. As anyone with intelligence can see that is a substantial difference."

This speaker does not give the audience even a faint clue as to whether the figure went up, down or sideways. He also fails to provide the audience with either paper, pencil or time. Then he bases a profound conclusion on this:

"On the basis of these figures it is obvious that we must change our foreign policy."

I have never quite been able to make up my mind as to whether this arithmetical abracadabra type of performance is best classified as "applied" stupidity or "creative" stupidity; however the adjective is not too important.

If you are going to use figures—*you do the arithmetic*. Tell the audience the results whether they are increases or decreases etc.—use round numbers that illustrate the order of magnitude involved and the point you are trying to make. If you must, have the alleged exact figures available on a hand-out sheet. When you are speaking don't expect an audience to remember multi-digit box car numbers and do mental arithmetic. Most people can't even remember their own automobile license number, let alone add or subtract and do numerical gymnastics while they simultaneously listen.

ILLUSTRATIONS

Whether we are saints, sinners, scholars, scientists, students or scullery maids, we learn by our senses. Seeing, hearing, tasting, smelling, feeling, and touching are the receiving apparatus by which we obtain the communication on which we base our learning. Depending on what we are learning, the percentage of reception by each of our senses varies.

For example, sight, taste and smell are very heavily involved in learning to enjoy eating food but much less involved if you were learning about the world's food supplies. This you learn through hearing and seeing, listening and reading.

Figures vary as to how much we learn by listening (10 to 20%) and by seeing (60 to 80%). Regardless of how these figures vary, the evidence is overwhelming that any time you can combine sound and sight you are compounding the maximum percentage in favor of learning. You greatly increase the probability that your remarks will be understood and remembered.

Any speaker can make his talk much more entertaining, and have his points better understood and longer remembered, if he will use some simple visual examples.

While it is true that what people hear may go in one ear and out the other, what people see seldom goes in one eye and out the other.

No one has ever disputed the wisdom of the Chinese proverb that "one picture is worth a thousand words." Yet very few speakers take advantage of visual techniques. And most of those who try use such elaborately bad visuals that they defeat themselves and their ideas.

Have you ever endured the applied stupidity of full pages of solid typing being projected on a screen, all the typing too small to read by anyone including the speaker? Or the charts showing crowded tables of figures in faint microscopic reproduction that project instant statistical stupidity? Or the mentally barren bore who reads his slides to you line by painful line? I always presume the point he is trying to illustrate is that he can read fine print, if given enough time.

How about the so-called economic graphs whose technicolor lines crisscross in a thousand ways, looking as if they were made by a drink-crazed chicken chasing a sex-crazed spider alternately across an ink pad and some mildewed graph paper?

The speaker usually explains that although you can't see it, if you could see it, this chart "would clearly illustrate that the rate of decline in growth for the preceding fiscal year, probably exceeded the growth in the rate of decline for the calendar year if you made adjustments for the increase in the declining rate of acceleration."

Visuals that don't visualize insult the intelligence of any audience. The person who inflicts poor visuals on an audience should be sentenced to watch day-time television for life. If visuals don't illustrate the point with abundant clarity, and if they are not simple, they should not be used with a talk.

Obviously there are visuals which are excellent for use in books, magazines and other printed material, but are worthless when used with a live presentation and vice versa.

Presumably, the person reading a book, technical or professional journal, can pause—take time out—study the graph. He can even check it out with some figuring on a scratch pad before he procedes at his own pace.

The listener cannot do this. He must get the point on the fly and mentally move on when the speaker verbally procedes to the next point.

If you must show a page of figures, subdue all lines except one. Then magnify that line so that it can be easily read. Point out that this line illustrates the basic point further illustrated by the rest of the figures shown (legible copies of this slide can be available as handouts).

Much better than figures are cartoons illustrating your points with humor, satire or vivid reality. For example, you might want to illustrate that in your business things do not always measure up to outward appearances with a simple optical illusion like this:

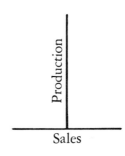

(both lines are the same length)

With a little applied imagination, almost any important point can be made or vividly reinforced with a simple cartoon. For example, a picture of the carrot and the stick can illustrate one kind of motivation and a picture of a salesman with a blow torch applied to the seat of his pants can illustrate another kind of motivation.

Some of the most effective of all visuals are simple everyday things like an electric motor, a ladder, or a window.

For example, you can point out an idle electric motor is as useless as a salesman sitting in the home office—it won't work until someone turns on the current and gets some action.

Ladders can be used to illustrate many business principles. For example, you can point out that no one can go up the ladder of success until he develops enough confidence to take his foot off the step on which he is now resting.

A common window can be used to illustrate that many people have a great dream but like the kid looking in a candy store window, they won't realize their dream until they learn how to circumvent invisible barriers.

Relativity can be vividly illustrated with three basins of water at substantially different temperatures. If you put your hand in the hot water, but then move it to the lukewarm water, the lukewarm water will feel cool by comparison. However, if you start with your hand in the cold water and then move your hand to the lukewarm water, the lukewarm water would feel hot in comparison. One of the simplest objects that makes an excellent example of the function of leadership is a large rubber band. Point out that unless you put your tension on it, it will serve no useful purpose, but if you put too much tension on it, it breaks. A good sales manager is the guy who knows how much tension is enough.

If a point is worth making it is worth illustrating with either a verbal or visual illustration.

CHAPTER SEVEN

Trigger Your Mind

Having organized your ideas and having familiarized your-self with a lot of different ways of expressing these ideas, it is now time to develop a good set of notes based on trigger words. With a good set of notes it is difficult to make a bad presenta-tion. On the other hand, with a bad set of notes it is difficult to make a good presentation. Generally speaking, the briefer your notes are, the better.

Here's how to develop excellent notes. Once again spread out your 3x5 "idea cards," in numerical sequence. Review the idea or concept outlined on each card. Then select a single word that

31285

would trigger that idea in your mind. For example, your card might read like this:

---

constantly rising taxes create

constantly rising costs—not

subject to reduction

The one word that might trigger that concept in your mind might be "constantly" or "rising" or "taxes." Select whichever one of these words triggers that total idea in your mind. No one can select the right trigger word for another person; it is a do-it-yourself project. The appropriate trigger word for one individual is not necessarily the word which will trigger another individual's memory.

Let's assume that you have now decided "rising" is the word that triggers your memory. It mentally turns on that idea like a light switch turns on a light. Now take a colored pen or felt-tip marker and boldly print your trigger word on the reverse blank side of the card. The bolder and brighter the better.

Go through your idea cards, carefully selecting the best trigger word for each concept. Sometimes your first selection of a trigger word will be "ok"; sometimes it will take a good deal of trial and error to get the one word that will trigger your mental recollection of the idea. Whether it comes easy or hard, persist until each of your idea cards is identified with a trigger word. Test the validity of your choices by reviewing your idea cards, first looking only at the side of the card which has the trigger word on it. Each time you look at a trigger word see if you can immediately start discussing the idea outlined on the other side of the card. If necessary, refresh your memory by looking at both sides; then go through the cards again, this time reversing the process. Look at the outline and see if your mental reflex immediately recalls the trigger word. When you have confidence, convert your trigger words into a set of notes. Even if you have as many as 30 cards, your notes need only be 30 trigger words. Take a single sheet of paper and boldly and brightly print your trigger words one under the other in the proper sequence, like this—

RISING

PRODUCTION

DESIGN

RESEARCH

In an instance where a concept has dual, inter-related, but separate ideas such as:

Personnel Programs
(a) training of technical worker
(b) development of supervisor and executive
     personnel

You may want to add secondary words. In this case the idea card might read:

PERSONNEL   TRAINING   DEVELOPMENT

Since you are only going to speak about subjects with which you are thoroughly familiar, you will find this trigger word technique very easy to achieve. It has a number of advantages over a complete, or semi-complete text. It gives you time to look at your audience, make eye contact and note the audience reaction. Responding to this audience feed-back, you can expand or contract your discussion of any point you wish to make. Unlike the paper-reader, you are not mentally confined to a straight-jacket of your own making. You will also find that one-word notes are far more effective than notes consisting of phrases and sentences.

> When I develop my own talks I dictate my trigger words into a tape recorder at about three-second intervals. I then play the recorder and try immediately responding to each trigger word, with the gist of the idea card corresponding to that trigger word.

> By about the third run-through, I develop a conditioned reflex response between the trigger word and the corresponding idea. Occasionally, when the response does not come, I find it necessary to get a better trigger word.

Notes based on trigger words are most important to your success. At the risk of some duplication, I would like to summarize and re-emphasize some of these points.

If you are being presented as a knowledgeable person on the subject about which you are speaking, you should not read a prepared paper. It creates a credibility gap of your own making. Obviously, if you have to read about your speciality, word-for-word, you are not familiar with it and probably you are not an expert. Any high school student could read the same paper on the same subject as well or better, and he would not have to be an expert in anything except reading. A capable but occasional speaker should know how to speak effectively from notes based on trigger words. A capable professional speaker should not even use notes any more than a professional artist should paint by the numbers.

MAJOR AND MINOR POINTS

Obviously some of the points you will make are sufficiently complex to require sub-divisions into minor points which modify them. For example, if your major point was personnel, minor points might be executive, administrative, production. As a result, in your trigger word note format you would have major and minor trigger words.

For example, a personnel man who knows his business and has done his homework ought to be able to give a good luncheon talk with a set of notes like these 15 words, on one 5x8 card or piece of paper:

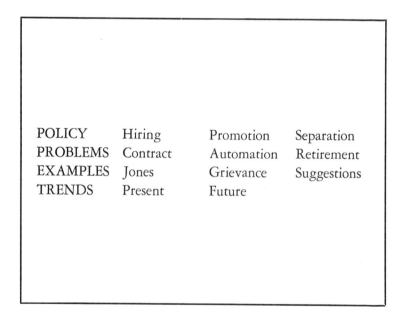

POLICY	Hiring	Promotion	Separation
PROBLEMS	Contract	Automation	Retirement
EXAMPLES	Jones	Grievance	Suggestions
TRENDS	Present	Future	

This system works beautifully if you will take the time and trouble to select the exact trigger word. For example, say "taxes" to a businessman and listen to him blast off for half an hour.

CHAPTER EIGHT

Make It Newsworthy

When he speaks at a meeting every business executive or professional man always has an "unseen" audience—that is, the people who will hear about his talk, even though they did not attend the meeting. They will form an impression of him and his organization. The unseen audience may be only those who read the minutes of the meeting, or it may be as vast as 30 million people who hear an excerpt or quote on a TV newscast, or read an account in the daily press, trade press, professional journals and other publications.

This unseen audience may not only be bigger than the audience at the meeting, but it also may be more influential. It can include government regulatory agencies, organized consumer groups, customers, union officials, legislators, or potential big industrial users. Such publicity provides an unlimited opportunity for you to project a favorable image of yourself and your organization. No amount of money can buy advertising as effective as space on the front page and mention on prime time news broadcasts.

Whether the people reading about you or hearing about you get a favorable reaction will depend not so much on what you said, but on what they *thought* you said. In turn, what the public thought you said will be conditioned by the echo of your condensed remarks as carried by the news media.

Under these circumstances, obviously you should help the news media get the brief, concise, accurate excerpts that they want and need. Every executive and professional who speaks should realize that whether he gets good, bad or indifferent publicity is about 99 per cent dependent on how he and those handling the meeting cooperate with the press. But as the speaker you should realize that frequently the publicity chairman or person assigned to handling the news media for a business or professional meeting has had no qualifying experience. This inexperience can inadvertently create poor coverage by the news media.

Unless a speaker is exceptionally prominent or highly controversial, he should not be so naive as to expect reporters to attend the meeting in order to cover his talk. News media people are engaged in an everlasting game of "beat the clock," meet the deadline. If they attend the meeting in order to cover your remarks they may not have time to work up the material fast enough to meet their deadline.

Always have the courtesy to send the news media a digest of the talk well in advance of the meeting, but with the release dates as of the day of the meeting. This material you send to the press is very important. If you want the papers to give you little or no coverage send out the full text of the talk, single spaced, typed on both sides of the page. Either no one will have time to boil it down to space limitation, in which case it won't get printed at all, or a few paragraphs will be extracted at random and possibly quoted out of context.

If you want to project a competent image, send a well-written, highly condensed digest to the news media. Also, tell them that the full text will be made available, *if they want it* (they very seldom do). Write your press digest in succinct newspaper style. Start with something interesting. If possible, tie it to some local event of current interest. Keep it brief, double spaced, and leave wide margins. The more easily your material can be used with the least amount of rewriting, editing or condensing, the more likely it is to be used. Remember you have more time, know more about the subject, and have a greater interest in the subject than a reporter does. If you, with your background knowledge and sustained familiarity with the subject cannot write a digest (when you are not hard pressed by a deadline and don't have to simultaneously write six other newsworthy stories), why in the world should you expect a reporter to do so? He does not have your background information, usually he is not familiar with the subject and he is hard pressed to cover other meetings, assorted murders and some newsworthy sex scandals, meet all his deadlines, and keep the boss off his back. In addition, he knows he will never win a pay raise or a Pulitzer prize for his coverage of your talk at that meeting.

The person who fails to have the courtesy to provide a press digest in advance of the meeting, and then screams that he was misquoted, has a mentality comparable to the juvenile delinquent who murdered his parents then demanded mercy from the judge because he was an orphan.

The secret of working successfully with the news media people involves exactly the same technique as working successfully with anyone else. Adapt your actions to an intelligent appreciation of the other fellow's viewpoint, professional limitations and business problems.

Like yourself and your associates, competent news people crave the psychic satisfaction of doing a good job, they take pride in their work. In their profession time pressure is a constant way of life and instant priority decisions a matter of economic survival. Unlike the automobile manufacturers, they cannot recall yesterday's product for adjustments and corrections.

Just as your ability to produce a quality product depends on the quality of raw material available to you, so does the news media's ability to produce a quality product depend on the raw material available to them. However, unlike you they have much less control over the raw material. While it is their job to edit your remarks, it is not their job to rewrite your material in order to make in interesting, or more understandable.

Remember the business of news media is to sell news. The only product it can sell is the news *that interests its particular readers.* Editors are constantly (almost desperately) searching for a daily supply of news, it is the raw material of their business. They welcome good, interesting press digests, because each day they have to select, edit and print or broadcast approximately the equivalent number of words in a 150,000 word book.

No matter how newsworthy your material is to you and your associates, if it isn't newsworthy to their readers or listeners, that particular news media can't use it. You cannot sell your material in the wrong market and neither can they. Probably because of regional prejudice, news about snowshoes is in more demand in Alaska than in Atlanta.

Therefore to make your release marketable, try to find a "news peg" to hang it on. Associate it with something which is currently in the news, for example: If three quarters of the way through your talk you examined and discussed ways of increasing profits by recycling and reclaiming waste products, in this age of ecology, your news peg for the daily press would be: "Mr. Doe told how waste products could be recycled thereby reducing pollution." (To the readers of the daily press increased profits would be secondary news.)

This means that you never start a release to the daily news media with a "lead line" that is of interest only to your "seen" audience. The lead line must capture the instant attention of the news media.

Remember, although you give away what you consider to be news, the news media has to sell news. As every businessman knows, it is frequently a lot easier to give away a poor product than it is to sell a good one. Your part in preparing a news release is to provide the news media with a quality product that can be sold, *to their particular customers,* at that time.

Honestly, accurately, and briefly tell—

Who
What
When
Where
How

Since you are not writing about a murder, it is desirable to provide your story to the news media before it happens so they don't have to handle it on a crisis basis. However, if for any reason your event is cancelled you have a moral responsibility to notify all news media *promptly*.

All news media receive a daily flood of non-sensational news releases of approximately equal news value. This deluge is in excess of the amount of material they can use. Some releases are so well prepared that they only require a lead line, others are so poorly prepared that they cannot be used unless they are substantially re-written. If you were the editor trying to beat a deadline, which material would you use? They make the same decision you would make.

The a,b,c's involved in making news are:

(a) If it isn't news, it should not be used.

(b) If it is interesting and brief, it most likely will be used, either in whole or in part.

(c) If it is merely interesting, but not brief, see "a" above.

As far as the daily news media is concerned, there just isn't enough time or professional talent available to re-work any news that isn't *sensational.* Therefore your release should be ready to print without rewriting.

TRADE JOURNALS AND NEIGHBORHOOD PRESS

Probably the most valuable and least appreciated resources of American business are the trade press, professional journals and business publications. Here is where the professional talks to the professional, where you have a true cross-fertilization of ideas among the elite of each profession and occupation. Be sure to include them in your press releases; also learn to use them as a resource for speaking material. As a rule they are not quite as hard pressed for deadlines, but they may or may not have the same intense competition for space.

Just as business publication and professional journals are interested in detailed information pertinent to the specialized interest of their audiences, most metropolitan areas have neighborhood and area daily, weekly and periodic publications that welcome news of *local interest.* It is the backbone of their circulation and economic survival. News of that PTA program, civic club speaker or social club happening which won't make two lines on page 69 in the big metropolitan daily may rate front page prominence in the Neighborhood News.

Every law-abiding citizen likes to see his name in the news. In the smaller local papers *names are news,* and names make circulation, circulation makes advertising, and advertising means the money which keeps the paper in business. Therefore, when preparing releases for smaller local news media, feature names —and get them right. If necesssary, attach a supplement, one sheet with a one- or two-line identification.

To summarize, remember these two things:

1. Unless you are involved in an illegal activity or a sensational news-making event, contact the news media, don't wait for them to call you.
2. Unless you are a dishonest person, don't try to swindle the the news media by submitting advertising disguised as news.

Here is a simple, practical, effective format for providing press digests to all types of media.

PRESS DIGEST

From Harper Valley PTA
For further information   *For* release

contact: _____   date: _____

address: _____   day: _____

phone: _____   time: _____

Remarks by John Doe*
at (business luncheon or dinner) meeting of (name of organization)

Title of talk _____

      Double space (8½x11 paper)
      block paragraphs
      wide margins
      start with an attention getting opening
      make it brief
      keep it newsworthy
      (Since it is a digest you need not use actual text word for word BUT YOU MUST HAVE IT ACCURATELY REFLECT THE ACTUAL TEXT)

* John Doe is (a couple of sentences indicating who John Doe is, where he is from, what is he known for, etc.)

CHAPTER NINE

Don't Get Booby-trapped

Unless you want to live dangerously and possibly project a ridiculous image of yourself, visit the meeting room prior to the start of the meeting. Paraphrasing immortal words that have been attributed to many different geniuses: "May the good Lord give you the intelligence to see what needs to be changed, the courage to insist on changing what can be changed and the fortitude to live with what cannot be changed"—or even the moral courage to cancel your talk.

The late Thomas E. Dewey, short in stature, was a serious contender for the presidency of the United States. On one occasion he was made to look utterly absurd when a sneak picture showed that he was standing on a wooden box in order to be tall enough to look over an obsolete non-adjustable lectern. That embarrassing picture not only haunted him throughout the campaign, but its harm was compounded by giving rise to the repeated observation that he looked like the little man on top of a wedding cake. Both the embarrassing picture and the degrading remark seriously damaged his public image.

In the opposite direction President Lyndon B. Johnson's image was not improved by the repeated pictures of him bent over like a question mark trying to read notes on a lectern that was too low for a man of his stature. Either of these gentlemen could, and should have, improved his image by the premature retirement of one or more appropriate members of his staff.

Consider the variety of handicaps I have encountered:

Lecterns without lights are commonplace.

Partitioned rooms are seldom if ever sound proof. On one occasion I was scheduled to speak at a business banquet in one-half of a partitioned ballroom on Saturday night in Norfolk. A little preliminary inquiry developed the fact that on the other side of that non-sound proof partition there was scheduled, for that same evening, a welcome home dance for a submarine crew returning from a one-year cruise.

Recently, at a national meeting, professional speakers notified the chairman that they would cancel the entire morning session rather than speak to 300 people in an auditorium designed to seat 3000. Had they been amateurs they probably would have tried to speak under these absurd conditions.

It is not unusual to have hotel sound systems break in with all kinds of anouncements throughout a speaker's talk because someone did not turn it off ahead of time.

In old hotels leaking pipes and noisy radiators are not unusual.

When a meeting place has a large room that can be partitioned into smaller rooms it is not unusual for loudspeakers in each section to be at a different sound level because they were independently adjusted when the rooms were used separately. Under these circumstances, when the total large room is used, the speaker sometimes cannot be heard in one part of the room, while his voice is so loud in another section of the room that he is rattling the fillings in people's teeth.

(See also CHECKLIST OF MEETING BOOBY-TRAPS, (page 118)

Many meeting-place managers are so accustomed to poorly run meetings that they welcome the individual or organization that not only knows what it wants but insists on getting it. It is always difficult for management to encourage employees to take pride in a good job when the customers are apparently thoroughly satisfied with slipshod service.

THE SOUND AND THE FURY

The one absolute "must" for every speaker is to try out the microphone prior to the start of the meeting and insist on getting it adjusted until it is approximately right for his voice (not someone else's voice). In an empty room an approximately right adjustment of the volume should sound slightly too loud, but have as little echo, or hollow sound, as possible. When you try out the mike, avoid the temptation to get too close or talk unusually loud. Test it realistically at a comfortable distance where you can find a degree of loudness that you can maintain for the duration of your talk.

A properly adjusted microphone merely magnifies your voice, it doesn't change it. If you mumble it mumbles louder, if you whisper it whispers louder. However if you speak clearly and distinctly it will probably speak loud and clear.

Always assume that some members of the audience are deaf and scattered around the room but anxious to hear you, so don't depend entirely on the microphone. Speak distinctly to your deaf friends and personally make eye contact as you do in every-day conversation. Let the microphone magnify your voice but don't expect it to do miracles and put out better than you put in. It not only won't do miracles it may not even do simple justice to your dulcet and/or stentorian tones.

Although modern man routinely visits the moon, science has yet to invent a typewriter that can spell correctly or a microphone that can enunciate clearly.

There is no such thing as a standard setting at which all voices will sound equally good. At a well-run professional meeting facility they will ask all the speakers on the program to test the sound system in advance of the meeting. They will then arrive at and make a record of the apparent optimum setting of the dials for each speaker's voice. While that speaker is being introduced, the dials will then be adjusted to his predetermined setting. After he begins speaking only minor adjustments will be made *if necessary*. There will be none of the electronic confusion which usually seriously interferes with the opening lines of each speaker on many programs.

No one can test a microphone for you any more than they can buy a pair of shoes that will fit your feet. Another person can test a microphone only to see if it is connected to the electricity and the sound system. Only you can determine how a microphone fits your voice. Did you ever attend a meeting where a masculine giant stands to speak and then his voice comes over the sound system bubbling like a teenage girl?

The microphone can be your greatest friend or worst foe. Check it out beforehand and *DON'T TAKE EVEN YOUR MOTHER'S WORD THAT A MICROPHONE IS WORKING AND PROPERLY ADJUSTED FOR YOUR VOICE.*

Try it out, have one of your friends roam about the room and listen in varying locations. Do not depend on an employee of the meeting place to tell you if it is adjusted for your voice.

> On one occasion I was trying out a microphone prior to the meeting. I was dissatisfied and constantly requesting adjustments, much to the annoyance of the manager of the hotel He was walking around the room supposedly auditioning the system; no matter what adjustments were made he repeatedly said "That's good." Fortunately, the sound man was persistent and took pride in his skill. Finally he made one more adjustment and for the first time my voice came through loud and clear. The hotel manager, without thinking, had a spontaneous reflex reaction, he boomed: "I'll be damned, that *really* sounds good, now."

* * *

> One day in a West Coast hotel we were trying to lick an echo in the front section of a ballroom that could be partitioned into three separate rooms. Finally we decided to shut off the front speakers in that one section since they were above, and even in back of the microphone, as the room was then set up. It developed that this system did not permit turning off individual speakers, so an obliging sound man got a tall ladder, climbed up, and cut the wires leading to those particular speakers. Immediately the echo stopped. Three years later I spoke in that same room, but to a smaller audience which was only using the front section of that same room.

This time the seating arrangement was reversed, and what had been the front of the room previously was now the back of the room. A preliminary trial indicated the sound system was completely unbalanced for this configuration and seating arrangement. Glancing upward I saw that the same speaker wires that had been cut three years before were still cut and unspliced, although hundreds of meetings had been held in that sectional room.

Next to airline timetables, and civil service job descriptions, one of the great works of fiction in America is that famous statement: "Don't worry about the sound—we always monitor the system." This can mean anything from an excellent painstaking professional job, to a bellhop, six stories away, occasionally looking at a dial when he is not otherwise engaged.

In Florida I visited a so-called sound control room set up to supposedly monitor four meeting rooms. In addition to the instruments which merely recorded loudness, not clarity, there also was a noisy air compressor, some elevator machinery and a deaf man who was watching a TV set, turned on full blast. He was the alleged monitor for which each meeting was paying a fee.

Unless you are so naive that you would buy a used car, sight unseen, from an out-of-town car dealer on a dark night, always test the sound system for your voice prior to the meeting.

Human nature is a peculiar thing, but all of us insist on doing the things at which we are least skilled the hard way. Conversely, when we do thing at which we are competent, we take advantage of all the help science and technology have to offer.

For example, almost all occasional speakers try to use a stand-up microphone which is the most difficult microphone to use, while all, or most all, professional speakers use a neck microphone which is the easiest microphone to use.

Everything about a stand-up microphone operates to the disadvantage of the non-professional speaker. Depending on which way a speaker turns, whether he raises or lowers his head, his voice goes up or down, or on and off, like a flickering candle in a draft. He leans forward to create the illusion of letting the audience in on a whispered confidence and his voice booms out like a train wreck of a hundred box cars loaded with T.N.T.

The speaker stands tall to take a firm stand, while his voice declines to a faltering whisper. If he glances too far left or right he frequently goes off the air. The speaker neither feels normal, looks natural, or is comfortable with that archaic device a few inches in front of his face. Of course, he cannot speak naturally because he is actually in a unnatural, awkward position. Meanwhile, from the viewpoint of the audience and the cameras, this archaic microphone not only blots out part of his face, but depending on how he moves, it appears to be an elongation of his nose or an extension of his ear. Frequently it appears to be the black space where his teeth used to be— before the accident.

The non-professional speaker should always insist on a neck microphone because it is a thousand times easier to use. It permits the speaker to be completely natural. No matter what motion he makes, the microphone remains the same distance from his mouth and the sound is uniform. He can raise or lower his voice on purpose, turn any way he pleases, and the volume of sound depends entirely on him and not on the way he is facing or the accidental distance between his mouth and the microphone. Because the speaker cannot see a neck microphone after he puts it on, it does not create an unnatural visual barrier between him and his audience. The audience not only looks natural to him but he even looks pretty good to them. There is no unnatural elongation of his nose or ears. He looks human.

If the meeting place tells you they don't have, or cannot provide a neck microphone, do not be astonished when you arrive to find that same meeting place lacks indoor plumbing facilities.

In my opinion, the fixed microphone is a technological tombstone constructed in memory of the electronics of 1920 when it replaced Rudy Vallee's megaphone.

In conclusion, unless you are determined to be your own worst enemy, do three simple things:

1. Thoroughly check out the meeting facilities prior to your appearance on the program.

2. Insist on personally checking out the sound system; not only to see if it is turned on, but more importantly, so you can get it adjusted to reflect your voice at its best.

3. Insist on having a neck microphone—not one that you can hold in your hand, but one that hangs around your neck on a cord out of sight and out of mind.

CHAPTER TEN

Getting to Know You

It is a well-known fact that statues and people seldom feel the same way about pigeons. People and statues get introduced to pigeons in different ways and this influences their reactions.

The whole point of an introduction is to influence the viewpoint of the audience. Contrary to popular practice, the audience is probably not interested in your biography from childhood to manhood or possibly not even from infancy to adultery. They don't care how many brothers and sisters you had; what elementary schools you attended, or even if all your ancestors were married. Generally speaking, most audiences think that degree of boring detail should be saved for a more pertinent purpose such as your *obituary*. Many a speaker who receives an obituary introduction lives up to the occasion by dying on his feet.

An introduction should highlight your qualifications, not bury them in detail. When you are speaking on a business subject, the fact that you have thirteen children is relatively unimportant. However, if you were speaking at a Planned Parenthood Meeting, the fact that you had thirteen children would be significant. Details about elementary schooling are not pertinent unless you are speaking at a home-town class reunion.

The more years you have been out of school, the less emphasis your introduction should place on your previous schooling, much of which is now oboslete. If you are 24 years old, emphasis on your scholastic preparation is significant because you have not yet had time to demonstrate your competence by performance; but if you are 46 years old, emphasis on your demonstrated performance and your recent accomplishments is much more significant than what you allegedly studied more than a generation ago.

The prime purpose of a speaker's introduction is to establish his right to speak on that subject (his qualifying experience) and to assure the audience that he will be interesting and well worth listening to. Anything which does not contribute to establishing the qualifications, interesting personality, or competence of the speaker in terms of that audience's interest is irrelevant. It is significant that the entire correct introduction for the President of the United States is:

> "Ladies and gentlemen—
> The President of the United States"

When the chairman of the meeting asks for a copy of your biography he is using a figure of speech. He probably doesn't want your complete biography any more than he would expect you to give a detailed medical history in answer to his courteous inquiry "How are you?"

Any effective introduction should be typed double-spaced in large type on one side of one sheet of paper. If you have to submit a longer introduction, you probably are not important enough to be on the program. Preferably it should have been typed on a speech typewriter, in type so heavy that the nearsighted chairman of the meeting can read it in the dim glow of a flickering lectern light. Lectern lights are made by the same company that makes the lights used to illuminate taxicab meters.

A speaker should always carry spare copies of his introduction and have an extra copy readily available for the chairman who cannot find the one which was mailed to him, or who left the copy you gave him earlier in his hotel room. Frequently, representatives of news media will also request copies of your introduction.

All experienced speakers could write a tragic comic book about the introductions they have had. It is amazing how many people of sufficient background to preside at a meeting have never learned how to introduce a speaker—either what to say, or how to say it. Their errors run from bad grammar to very bad manners.

Some examples—

The would-be comedian who was called on to introduce me. He arose and talked for forty-five minutes. During this time he read a number of jokes including the punch lines. He broadcast his disorganized personal opinions on a wide variety of subjects, then finally sat down, forgetting to introduce anyone.

The State Senator who used up thirty minutes of the speaker's time with side-splitting anecdotes about ridiculous and rude introductions he had personally received. He then proved he could give as well as he could receive. At the end of 30 minutes his entire introduction was: "I guess it is now time for our speaker; here he is."

The thoughtless people who don't have the courtesy to personally meet or talk to the speaker before introducing him. Frequently, they have not even looked over the material they are going to mumble.

The mentally clumsy people who ad-lib inept comments. On one occasion I listened to an excellent, brief, informative introduction of a distinguished banker. It ended by stating that he was the Vice-President of a nationally important bank. Unfortunately, the chairman then down-graded himself and the speaker with the anti-climatic: "Of course, at his bank, vice-presidents are a dime a dozen."

The backwoods boob who is a hold-over from the illiterate days of frontier America. He believes it is his job to insult and ridicule the speaker with his semi-brillant wit, such as:

"If I had my way we wouldn't have speakers at this meeting."

"I never heard a speaker yet that wasn't full of bull."

"I was given this material to use in introducing the speaker, but I am not going to waste your time and my time reading that ?!X."

"Son, we paid you and you have to speak, but damned if we have to listen to you."

The confused chairman who refuses to use notes. He gets all the facts right about a speaker; but unfortunately, those facts relate to a speaker other than the one scheduled to stand up and talk.

The deadly and dangerous chairman who completely fails to get order or attention before introducing the speaker. With no one listening, he gets up, introduces the speaker, and then sits down. It then becomes necessary for the speaker to do both of the chairman's jobs:

1. Get order
2. Introduce the speaker

Any up-coming young person, executive or professional person who prides himself on breeding and potential should learn the etiquette of properly introducing a speaker. This is not only one time you may read a paper, it is one time you probably should *read*. It is your job to do two things:

1. Get order and absolute attention

2. Project an image of the speaker as a competent, interesting person who is abundantly qualified to speak on the chosen subject. How good you are depends on how effectively you establish a friendly, attentive relationship between the speaker and the audience, before he begins to speak.

CHAPTER ELEVEN

You're On Your Own!

Paste this on your mirror the morning of your talk:

When you speak, speak loud and clear. Pretend there is a deaf man in the last row. Talk to the people, not to the mike. Make eye contact with them. You would not talk to a friend wihout looking at him; the audience is made up of your friends. They want you to succeed. And you can do it!

—Joe Powell

Let's start with the assumption that you have survived the introduction and are now on your feet, ready to talk. Like the mosquito at the nudist camp, you know what to do; your dilemma is where to start.

Never forget Newton-Powell's law:

"A mind at rest remains at rest—until some mind-stretching speaker puts it in motion."

As a speaker, your job is to be so interesting that you will trick people into thinking without knowing it. But unless you are a professional comedian, don't open your talk with the traditional irrelevant joke. Whenever I attend a meeting and the speaker opens with a forced joke, memorized or painfully read, I know an amateur hour is about to begin.

What is the purpose of an opening? It does not have anything to do with comedy. The purpose of your opening is to:

Get the absolute undivided attention of the entire audience in the shortest possible time.

Anything that interferes with that objective is a mistake.

The quickest, easiest way to achieve a good opening is:

1. Remain silent until you have absolute quiet. If you don't have quiet, sit down and give the chairman a second chance to do what he should have done.

2. Open with a *very loud* challenging question that personally involves each member of the audience.

Such as:

What odds will you give me that you will be alive in the year 2000?
What is your basis for those odds?

Have you thought about it?

What are your odds on being employed next year, 5 years from now?
What are you doing about your future?

Is your organization going to be in business this time next year?

How long do you expect to live?
Why?

A professional speaker can open with a whisper, but the occasional speaker should open so forcefully that he absolutely and unquestionably dominates the room. Nobody else should be allowed to hear themselves think! Then, as you get complete attention, you can taper off on the volume.

Of course, a good opening can be an attention-getting anecdote that immediately grabs the audience. The greatest opening I ever heard was:

"One year ago tonight, I was a drunken bum lying in the gutter."
"Tonight! one year later, I am a thirty-thousand-dollar-a-year executive!

This got undivided, instantaneous attention!

To repeat, the purpose of your opening remark is not to amuse the audience, not to entertain them. *Its only purpose is to get complete undivided attention in the shortest possible time.*

Whatever you do, always know thoroughly your opening sentence and your closing sentence *without having to refer to any notes.* Do you know of a sadder sight than a political candidate who has to read—"I am very glad to be here tonight in the beautiful city of _____" Then he fumblingly turns the page, so he can read what city he is happy to be in. It happens every four years.

Once you have an audience, never, never, let them go until the conclusion of your talk. Above all, don't practice that do-it-yourself applied stupidity of the speaker who finally has attuned the audience to his wave length and like an old-time express train he is high-balling down the track to his destination, but at the moment he elects to tell a funny story completely unrelated to his message. As a result, the minds of the audience are side-tracked, the speaker returns to the main line, but he leaves his audience on the siding.

APOLOGIES ARE NOT IN ORDER

Never, never open a talk with an apology. Don't tell the audience you consider yourself a poor speaker. Let them decide for themselves; they may or may not agree with you. Above all, never say that the subject is not one with which you are familiar. If that is true you should have declined. And don't explain you did not have time to prepare. If that is true you should have cancelled your appearance. No one has the moral right to waste the time of an entire roomful of people.

> An ineffective speaker who, over a period of years, speaks 200 times to an average audience of 500 people has in effect killed the working lifetime of a single individual (50 years × 200 hours = 100,000 hours). He should be tried for murder!

The speaker who starts with an apology is like the surgeon who, thinking out loud, lets the semi-conscious patient overhear a soliloquy like this—"Well! well this is news to me. The chart says it is an appendectomy, I thought it was supposed to be another ingrown toe nail operation. I haven't removed an appendix for quite some time, but I guess it will come back to me after I start operating. We will muddle through—somehow."

TO READ OR NOT TO READ

Up to now, I have assumed that you are never going to read a talk. Why? Among the tens of thousands of skilled actors in America you will be hard pressed to name ten who give readings. Yet many businessmen and professional people, who make no claim to being skilled actors, are determined to read their talks aloud. They have seldom, if ever, acquired any skill in reading aloud and usually their only experience in reading

aloud to an audience has been confined to reading bed-time stories to their very young children. These experiences have not been unqualified successes; usually the children have had to interrupt and correct them: "No daddy, that isn't what the little bear said." In addition, the amateur reader frequently succeeded in putting himself to sleep even before he put his audience to sleep. Few mortals achieve the dynamic dullness of the alleged speaker who routinely reads his prepared paper to a defeated audience.

There are people who can read aloud brilliantly, but they are not amateurs. And the material they read has not been composed by other amateurs. The average business executive reading a prepared talk is as exciting as listening to a beginning child violinist playing a solo that was composed by another beginner.

One of the sad sights in America is to watch the pathetic performance of an otherwise capable executive as he stumbles his way through a public reading. He even methodically reads what is supposed to be a funny story and then has to turn the page to mechanically read the punch line.

With three exceptions, a business or professional man should not plan on reading his talk *unless he has had professional training and experience.* The three exceptions when an amateur may read are:

1. He is delivering a statement of national policy and the fate of nations hangs on every word.
2. His audience is made up of illiterates who could not read the talk if he mailed it to them.
3. He is posing as an expert on a subject with which he is unfamiliar.

In this latter case he should especially read a paper. The audience will then blame his poor presentation on his lack of reading ability, rather than on his lack of knowledge of the subject matter.

Politicians may read their talks for different reasons:

1. Some have had so much professional experience that they can be very effective.
2. Some need to make several talks on different subjects to different audiences in close sequence.
3. Some need to demonstrate to their constituents that they can read.

If you insist on reading, remember this: to be effective your text must be written in the dialect of spoken English, not written English. Few people can write spoken English. See Appendix II, Page 121

SHOWMANSHIP—REAL AND PHONEY

Under appropriate circumstances a little honest showmanship is in order. It can help dramatize your message so that it will be remembered and it can project an even more favorable image of the speaker. However, don't overdo it, and don't fake it like the gay 90's small time court house politicians used to do.

> At one time I knew one of these phonies. Whenever he had a speaking engagement he wasted a tremendous amount of his and everybody else's time preparing, memorizing and rehearsing his talk. When he was introduced he would stride to the lectern conspicuously carrying a thick stack of typed pages which gave everyone reason to believe they were going to sit through the reading of a very long, very dull speech. To further the illusion, he would start a miserable stumbling reading of the first page. About half way through the second page he would become visibly disturbed, look up and say: "This is the speech my staff prepared. Obviously they don't understand people like you—I am not going to waste your time. I am not going to read that canned tripe to you. I am going to honestly share my thoughts with you and speak from my heart."

> Then conspicuously flinging his supposedly prepared speech to the floor with visible disgust, he would proceed with faked spontaneity to deliver the talk that had been so carefully prepared, endlessly rehearsed and painstakingly memorized. Before leaving the lectern, during the thunderous applause for his presumably spontaneous remarks he was always careful to retrieve the counterfeit speech he had thrown to the floor.

The next time you see a speaker toss a so-called prepared speech to the floor, try to pick it up before he does. It might make interesting reading.

BUTTERFLIES—INEBRIATED OR SOBER

Audiences are like mirrors—they reflect the speaker's image. If he doesn't like them they won't like him; if he is nervous they will become nervous; but if he is enjoying the experience so will they.

According to my publisher it is immoral, illegal and indecent to publish anything about speaking without discussing the varieties of butterflies which allegedly live, thrive and fly in speakers' stomachs.

Butterflies like leprechauns must first exist in your mind before they can play pranks on you.

If a person claims he has never had butterflies, he probably has missed a normal healthy human experience. However, if a person alleges he suffers swarms and swarms of butterflies before speaking, he needs a mental tune up. When you get those butterflies out from under the mental magnifying glass they no longer look or feel like fire-snorting, smoke-breathing, flying dragons. In proper perspective they are as pretty and as harmless as technicolor pansies.

Butterflies, like other forms of worry, are created when we reverse our imagination and use it negatively to create fear, instead of using it positively to create confidence.

The imagination that can generate quantities of fear when you let it project a mental picture of failure, is the same imagination that generates equal quantities of continuing confidence when you use it to picture yourself succeeding.

Whether your imagination is your friend or foe mainly depends on whether you use it positively (constructively) or negatively (destructively). Imagination is a continuously running mental process, man's most versatile tool; but like any other tool it can be used constructively or misused destructively. Man can control imagination to his advantage or let it run uncontrolled to his disadvantage.

Your imagination is something like a computer—it doesn't care what you put into it, but what comes out will be as good or as bad as what you put into it. The computer axiom applies—

$$GI = GO$$
Garbage in = Garbage out

In order to attune your imagination constructively, to generate confidence for speaking, you only have to do five simple things:

1. Be prepared
2. Be prepared
3. Be prepared
4. Be prepared
5. Be prepared

In speaking or any other activity nothing generates confidence like the self-knowledge that you are throughly prepared to succeed.

Preparation creates confidence
Confidence produces success
and
Success breeds more success

Since for years you have been successfully conversing in small groups, you can obviously talk successfully to a larger group—even though it happens to be called an audience! The difference is psychological, rather than real. The speaking principles are the same and the techniques of presentation vary only moderately. Therefore, since most executives routinely and effectively talk to groups, they can very readily learn to talk with equal effectiveness to audiences.

Follow the steps outlined in this book and in the BNA film: "Unaccustomed As They Are." Do your homework before you get up to speak, stack the odds in your favor by:

Only saying yes to the right audience.
Have a good message.
Say it with interest and humor.
Enjoy doing it.

If you imagine you have a surplus population of butterflies, take an aspirin. It will not only relax you, it will cause the butterflies to take a siesta. However, don't take a cocktail or other alcoholic drink for at least a couple of hours before speaking. There is no truth in the superstitution that alcoholic spirits will appease butterflies. If you think sober butterflies are annoying, wait until you experience inebriated butterflies. They do stunt flying in formation, have aerial combats, practice crash landings, launch missiles, drop bombs and organize non-scheduled shuttle flights between the speaker's brain, kidney and bowels.

The hazards of drinking and driving are well known, unfortunately not enough people are aware of the hazards of drinking and speaking. While cocktails in moderation may improve the receptivity of the audience, they never improve the quality of the speaker's transmitter. Because of the normal tenseness of a speaker, the drink that might be merely relaxing can unexpectedly become an embarrassing alcoholic lubrication that frequently converts a dry wit into a liquid loud mouth.

Speaking effectively involves mental acuity. A speaker continuously coordinates the gears of his mind with the machinery of his mouth, constantly converts silent thinking into articulate words. Occasionally he will quite naturally make a slip of the tongue, just as all of us do in everyday speech. It doesn't bother an individual in everyday conversation and it should not bother a speaker, unless he has had a drink. However, if he had had even one or two moderate drinks he probably will become overly concerned about that slip-of-the-tongue, and instinctively tense up, slow his rate of speaking and become boring. On the other hand, if a speaker had had too many drinks, his talk is likely to become a prolonged slip of the mind, leaving the audience wondering if he is unable to handle his drinks or if he is getting senile. Neither image helps him or his organization. In fact, career-wise it frequently indicates that he has already gone about as far as he can go.

An excellent rule to follow is never drink before speaking.

FAST OR SLOW?

Try an experiment—think of nothing, for one minute. In fact you can't think of nothing for 10 seconds or even 5 seconds. The more intelligent you are the more impossible it is to think of nothing. Although there are some stupid people who can't think intelligently, even stupid people find it very difficult to think of nothing. No person with a normal I.Q. can think of nothing as long as he is awake, conscious, and sober.

Therefore, the more intelligent an audience is, the more likely it is for their minds to wander if a speaker doesn't present a succession of ideas fast enough to command continuous sustained attention. Did a slow speaker ever put you to sleep? You have two choices, either you go to sleep or start thinking of something else that will sustain your interest.

Competent executives can listen faster than most occasional speakers can talk, and much faster than an amateur can read. While there are not too many people who read faster than 200 to 300 a words a minute, most executive, professional and technical people find it impossible to listen that slowly unless the speaker is exceptionally dramatic, with an actor's flair for showmanship that compels constant audience attention. Seldom does an occasional speaker need to worry about slowing down, unless he is slurring his words or has a speech impediment. His problem is to go fast enough to maintain interest.

BE PREPARED TO CUT

In preparing a talk always predetermine what part can be dropped if you get pressed for time. Since, due to unrealistic planning, most programs run late, the further down you are on the program the more likely you are to have to cut, or at least telescope your remarks.

For example, the meeting scheduled to start at 8:30 A.M. won't actually start until about 9:00 A.M., if you are lucky. Just as a meeting scheduled to start at 9:00 doesn't start until 9:30 A.M.

When the people have stayed overnight at a hotel where the meeting is held, the hotel simply cannot absorb the impact of all these people wanting breakfast simultaneously about one-half hour before the meeting is scheduled to start. Similarly, if people are driving to the meeting that morning at rush hour, it is inevitable some will be delayed in traffic and in parking. So the first speaker starts late and sometimes also runs overtime. In all probability the program shows a scheduled 10 to 15 minute coffee break. No matter what the program says, that coffee break will take about 25 to 30 minutes. Of necessity coffee breaks are also kidney breaks.

One way or another, if you were originally scheduled to be introduced at 11:15 you are doing well if you get introduced by 11:30 A.M. More likely, it will be 11:45 A.M. If you were originally allowed 45 minutes from 11:15 to 12 noon, you now have 15 minutes. Maybe you can go to 12:15 P.M.; but your 45 minute talk now has to be done in 30 minutes.

As a banquet speaker, you should always try to be introduced at the earliest possible moment after the waiters have left. You can expect, however, that introduction of the head table, awards presentations, barber-shop quartets, etc. will precede you and could extend into the wee hours.

The moral: always plan a shorter talk than the time allotted to you, and even then be prepared to cut your remarks if necessary.

BE PREPARED TO STOP

The closing sentence of your talk is extremely important. An excellent speaker never drifts to a non-conclusive finish. His closing sentence should deliver a mental impact that will cause his message to be recalled and remembered. It can be a quotable quote, slogan, picturesque phrase or your message itself. Remember Patrick Henry's classic ending:

> I know not what course others may take; but as for me, give me liberty or give me death.

Patrick Henry concluded with a dynamic emotional statement of his message. Although your message may not justify the emotion-charged ending of a Patrick Henry, your message does require a "3-R" closing statement that *repeats, reinforces* and *reminds* the audience of your message.

Your closing sentence should be so succinct and so emphatic that it will leave no doubt in the audience's mind or in your mind that you have concluded your remarks. This concluding sentence should be so positive, so definite, that even a wound-up speaker won't be tempted to add one more word.

Thoroughly prepare and practice a definite decisive concluding sentence. Then use it!

CHAPTER TWELVE

And in Conclusion

If you get nothing else out of this book, please get engraved on your mind one thing, and never, never forget it: Once you start verbally communicating, and focusing on a specific target, never, never deviate by one single word, deed, thought or action. Success inevitably comes to those who know where they are going.

Learn to enjoy speaking, it is a lot of fun. The audience is on your side. Believe me, they want you to be good even more than you do. All they ask is that you don't insult them by opening with an apology or implying that they are so illiterate that you have to read to them.

If you have previously taken a high school or college course in public speaking by an English teacher who could not talk and therefore put all the emphasis on grammar, gestures and grooming, do not be too disturbed. In time you can overcome that misfortune.

In the final analysis, although you can learn a lot about swimming by reading books, seeing films and attending lectures, you cannot learn to swim unless you get in the water. This principle is true of speaking. My BNA film, this book and other books can help you learn about speaking, but none of these can teach you to speak. You cannot become a speaker unless you dive in and face an audience.

Join with a group of other "up and coming" speaking people who want to succeed. In the beginning practice on each other until you gain confidence among fellow beginners.

That's like swimming in the shallow end of the pool, but once you have gained enough confidence, head for the deeper water, the audience of strangers. But never forget practice does not make perfect unless you are doing something right. If you are doing it wrong and keep practicing, soon you will be able to do it perfectly wrong. First get the theory right then get the experience.

> Among the more dubious bits of advice given in many books on speaking is the sinister suggestion that would-be speakers should practice their talks in front of a mirror! If you want to become super-self-conscious, this method is guaranteed to produce results. If you hold a big enough sign in front of an audience they can read it. Now try holding a sign in front of a mirror and see if you can read it. A woman speaker may be able to practice in front of a mirror without too much damage to her ego since women are accustomed to seeing the unnatural, reversed, image of themselves which is reflected by a mirror. But most men make a limited use of mirrors and they're not at ease in front of a mirror except when shaving. Then men see their faces in a variety of reverse distortions and grimaces. (Which doesn't disturb them, since they know that when not shaving, their visage is debonnaire and ruggedly handsome.) Therefore men should never practice a talk in front of a mirror and destroy their personal masculine mystique.

Before you move up always get enough success and confidence that you can accept an occasional failure at the next level. Like the guy running hurdles on a track team, start with the low hurdles and only move to the high hurdles when you have enough confidence that you will not panic if you knock one down occasionally.

In speaking, as in learning to walk, occasionally you have to fall down in order to keep learning and succeed. Failing constructively is always part of the learning process.

To enjoy golf you do not have to be a professional. Speaking is the same—in order to enjoy speaking you do not have to be a professional speaker.

Although we lie politely to our children and tell them democracies are run by the majority, every sophisticated adult knows that it is not true. Democracies are run now, and always have been, by the articulate citizens. The articulate people run the country and it makes little difference if they are in the majority or in the minority.

If you want to be influential, learn how to speak. If you want to be a good citizen become articulate. Whether I agree with your beliefs and opinions is not nearly as important as whether you are an articulate citizen able to state your beliefs and opinions.

As an individual, you are unique. There is no one else on earth exactly like you. You owe something to the world: your individual viewpoint, how things look to you, your ideas. You are more important than you think you are.

Become an articulate citizen.

No matter whether your goal is learning to speak or something else, timetable your goal and never, never deviate. Do that and your eventual success is as inevitable and as certain as tomorrow's sunrise.

In the relatively few years since I figured that one out, I have had more fun, made more money, achieved more results, done more good and had more recognition and success than I previously had in 2/3 of a normal American lifetime.

If you elect to be an effective speaker, and if you are a moral person, you must learn two new commandments, the eleventh and the twelfth—they particularly apply to speakers.

11. Thou hast a moral responsibility *to knowest what thou art talking about.*

12. Thou shalt not waste the time of a single member of thy audience. Be thou witty, brief, interesting, and above all, informative. Thou needs not be dull in order to appear profound.

Planning and Producing Profitable Meetings

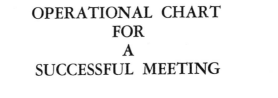

OPERATIONAL CHART
FOR
A
SUCCESSFUL MEETING

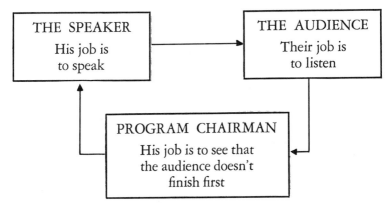

Let us assume that by the democratic process of election, or by the undemocratic process of the boss telling you *"To get with it,"* you have become program chairman of the upcoming meeting.

Whether you do it well, or poorly, the job will involve about the same amount of hard work, blood, sweat and tears. *As in most things failure takes no less work than success.* It merely takes a different orientation. Running a successful meeting does not depend nearly as much on whether you work hard as it does on whether you work intelligently.

This challenge presents you with a tremendous opportunity

to display your executive talent. Do it well and it will focus attention on your ability and your potential value to the organization. It can give you quite a head start in the competition for recognition and promotion. Do it poorly and the audience will not only turn off their hearing aids but they will also turn off their enthusiasm and motivation. Sometimes they also turn off their loyalty and respect for the organization.

> Ever talk to a salesman who has just attended a meeting where every speaker was a home-office executive making his once-a-year public appearance reading his non-motivating way through an amateurishly prepared speech written by his staff? Some of these speakers do a great job of *un*-selling. This executive is a thoroughly competent individual in his own specialty *which isn't speaking.* Prior to his sad personal performance at this annual meeting, everyone in the regional office was impressed when they heard from him or about him. Of course, when they leave this meeting, they may begin to wonder if he is as bright as they thought he was.
>
> Since there are certain subjects which can only be discussed by experts in these specialties within the organization, it is obvious that the presenter should be picked not only because of his ability to make an effective presentation. If necessary, back up the presenter with some technical experts to answer questions, rather than have the major presentation be dull.
>
> The company that cannot sell its own salesmen need not wonder why its salesmen cannot sell its products.

Good meetings don't happen by accident. They happen on purpose because they were properly programmed in four major areas, namely:

1. They have a specific purpose and a definite objective.
2. They provide both a proper physical and psychological environment consistent with the purpose of the meeting. Unless you believe the auto salesman who tells you the car was owned by an old lady who kept the car in the garage, don't believe glib people who tell you partitioned meeting rooms are sound proof.
3. They have articulate interesting speakers who can dramatize and verbally visualize the messages you want delivered.

4. They are programmed so that the speakers deliver their message in the most effective batting order.

CHOOSING SPEAKERS

All of these factors are controllable. "The right speakers in the right places on your program" will make your meeting most successful, just as the wrong speakers can wreck your meeting. Every speaker on your program either contributes to or detracts from the value and success of your meeting.

Despite brochures to the contrary, there is no such person as "The Best Speaker in America" or "America's #1 Speaker." Those claims are wishful thinking.

As far as your meeting is concerned, the best speaker is whatever competent speaker and articulate thinker has the ability to attune himself to your specific audience and effectively dramatizing the message you want delivered.

Speaking ability of every speaker varies with the subject about which he is speaking. That is why outstanding speakers do not speak on just any subject. They leave that dubious distinction to the amateurs. Outstanding speakers specialize on a limited number of themes. On these themes they become recognized authorities and on their specialty they are #1. This specialization permits an outstanding speaker to deliver many different talks, always on the subject in which he specializes. As a result his talks are consistently excellent, each sensitively attuned to the nature of the occasion, the purpose of the meeting, and the composition of the audience.

Just as the value of a tool depends on its particular suitability for the specific job that needs to be done, so also the value of a speaker depends on his particular suitability to the specific job that needs to be done. If you do not use a hammer to drive screws or tighten bolts, don't assume any one speaker is an all-purpose management tool. On a well-balanced program you may want one speaker to explain a complicated technical process, while you may want another to give an economic briefing, others to stretch minds, educate, entertain or explain company policy. Your best choice will always be the individual with competence in that area who also has the ability to attune to your audience and articulately deliver the message so that it will not be forgotten. Depending on the job that needs to be done, "The Best Speaker" could be anyone of a hundred effective speakers; however, it should never be an articulate speaker who is unfamiliar with his subject, or an expert on the subject who is inarticulate. Such speakers are as confusing as my neighbor who every summer sends his kid to camp and his dog to an obedience school.

Speakers from your industry or organization can deliver some messages that would not be accepted if they came from an outside speaker. However the reverse is also true. A professional speaker, from outside your organization, often can dramatize a message and gain a mental acceptance of the message when it could not be done by a spokesman from your own organization. All parents have had the frustrating experience of trying to get a "great truth" across to their youngsters only to have it receive zero acceptance. Then one night the same youngster comes rushing home to tell his parent the same great truth, only this time it was just told to him by some complete stranger.

Employees scheduled to attend a meeting with a total program of amateur speakers from their own company, usually look forward to it with all the enthusiasm that a young single fellow would have if he had to entertain his girl's mother while his girl went to the drive-in movies with another fellow. The better balanced programs usually involve speakers from within the organization and from outside the organization.

SETTING OBJECTIVES

Before a program chairman starts looking for prospective speakers that can make or mar his meeting, he should do two things:

1. Be sure that everyone involved in planning the meeting agrees on the specific purpose of the meeting, its goals and objectives.

For example, the company planning a sales meeting and the hotel where the meeting is being held both intend to work at making that meeting successful. However, what the company regards as a successful meeting is not necessarily what the hotel regards as a successful meeting. A sales meeting where all luncheons, dinners and cocktail parties were pleasant, enjoyable and profitable usually meets the hotel's success criteria.

From the company's viewpoint the social functions should be enjoyable etc. But what really matters is—did the salesmen become better salesmen, did they gain knowledge, develop increased company loyalty? In other words did they get personally and professionally motivated?

Many sales conventions hold thoroughly enjoyable convivial social affairs accompanied by dull business sessions where no one gets motivated. Some can pretty well be described by the old medical cliche—the operation was a success but the patient died.

Several times each year when I ask the purpose of a meeting I am told "We don't have a purpose, or a theme, we just have an annual meeting." Obviously if a meeting does not have a goal, it is impossible to tell whether it was successful. If you do not know where you are going, it is not only difficult to tell when you get there, you do not even know if you are headed in the right direction.

2. Determine the round-number cost *per meeting hour* of the meeting including the time of the audience, as well as the time of those planning the meeting and the cost of the facilities needed.

When you start thinking of meetings in terms of cost per meeting hour, you will become result oriented. *More importantly, you will also become value conscious.*

Having decided the total overall purpose of your meeting, then decide the purpose of each session such as: Is it primarily business, social relaxation, recreation or quasi-business and social, like a banquet or a luncheon? Contrary to corporate tradition, meetings with very serious purpose need not be boring, with an endless series of inexperienced speakers mumbling their weary way through an endless succession of dull papers. A competent speaker can make any subject interesting, even exciting. There are no interesting and dull subjects—only interesting and dull speakers.

A so-called "professional" speaker who routinely reads a prepared paper is obviously not a professional and should be shown the same respect that you would accord a professional artist who painted by the numbers.

A proper selection of speakers will make your investment pay off fantastically, while a poor selection will make your meeting an economic disaster. Considering the cost per meeting hour, the selection of speakers is not so much a matter of whether you can afford good speakers as it is a recognition of the fact that you cannot afford poor speakers. Regardless of whether you pay your speakers an honorarium or get him free, long-winded, mentally-disorganized, inarticulate mumblers, and dull paper-readers are all extremely expensive speakers. In terms of your cost per meeting hour you can't afford them even when you get them free!

All speakers, amateur and professional, come in a wide range of personal skill and subject competence. The speaker who was sensational at a business session may or may not be so hot at a banquet. Just as there are long distance runners and sprinters, there are speakers who can run an all day workshop and get better by the hour but who cannot deliver a forty minute talk. Similarly, there are speakers who are fabulous for short talks but who cannot run an all-day seminar.

Many people suffer from the dangerous illusion that all articulate writers are necessarily articulate speakers. Generally speaking, writers and speakers are two different breeds—one being articulate on his feet while the other is articulate on his seat, and seldom the twain shall meet.

Don't assume that because an individual is prominent, or has more academic degrees than a dog has fleas, that he is therefore necessarily a good speaker. He may or may not be a good speaker. Prominence and schooling are usually related to knowledge, but they are not related to speaking ability.

FINDING THE RIGHT SPEAKER

Speakers are usually located by the following four methods:

1. You hear one at a meeting you attended; or a business or professional colleague tells you about one he heard.

2. If you have already arranged for a speaker you know to be competent, or if you have heard a competent speaker, contact him and ask his recommendation about other speakers for your program.

The experienced professional not only knows who are the consistently competent speakers, he also knows the right and wrong program spots for some speakers. He can warn against the brilliant speaker who is sensational at a morning session, but who is susceptible to ice-cube poisoning at the cocktail party prior to the banquet at which he is to speak. All professional speakers give very serious thought to their recommendations because they know their reputations will be helped or hurt by the performance of people they recommend.

3. You can get interesting leads on speakers by consulting one of the many published rosters, directories or so-called encyclopedias of speakers. These lists usually contain background information such as name, address, phone number. In addition, with varying degrees of reliability they indicate such information as:

    When, where and how this speaker is available

    Subjects about which he speaks

    Financial consideration involved

    Experience

Generally speaking, there are three types of directories—

(a) Those you can buy such as the "Annual Dartnell Roster of Speakers" published by Dartnell Corporation, 4660 Ravenswood Avenue, Chicago, Illinois 60640. It contains an excellent variety of indexes, arranged geographically by subject matter, etc.

(b) Many trade association, business, executive, and professional groups publish directories of speakers for the benefit of their member organizations—such as the directories of

Sales and Marketing Executives International

National Management Association

Administrative Management Society

(c) Many organizations maintain, but do not publish, informal listing of speakers. Your trade, community or professional association may have such a list. Ask about it.

(d) Many business publications publish lists of business speakers with background information about their area of competence and availability such as the listings in:

Sales Meeting Magazine's Intl. Convention Facilities Directory

Sales Management Magazine

Columbia Books Publication "Trade and Professional Associations of the United States"

4. There are agents and agencies which promote and provide all kinds of speakers. Celebrities, radio-TV, and screen stars, prominent members of the press, prestigeous names, prominent people, and all kinds of socially acceptable speakers on every conceivable subject—community affairs, business, industry, education, child rearing, etc., etc.

In the agency recommendations and in the listings put out by various publications there is, unfortunately, a great variation in standards of quality governing the selection of individuals.

Some publications merely repeat whatever the speaker wishes to say about himself as long as he pays for the space involved. In others, he may not even be consulted and it is whatever somebody else wishes to say about him. He may not even know that he is listed, and the information may be misleading if not inaccurate. In the better listings, such as Dartnell and Sales Meetings Magazine, as with the better agencies, a speaker is not even considered until after he has submitted a substantial record of qualifying experience demonstrating his professional competence.

When time permits, it is always an excellent idea to audition a perspective speaker in action at another meeting.

Having discriminatingly developed a list of potential speakers for your program, contact them by phone (preferably) or by letter. A great deal can be told about a speaker by his reaction to your inquiry.

Every speaker, good, bad or indifferent, needs to know the date, time, place and financial considerations involved. However if he is the speaker you want he will also be equally interested in:

(a) The purpose of your meeting.

(b) The nature of the occasion.

(c) How you want his presentation to fit into your total program.

(d) Size and predominant personal characteristics that will provide a profile of your audience such as:

1. levels of responsibility
2. income variations and groupings
3. range of completed schooling
4. age variations and groupings

(e) What or who precedes or follows him on the program, and the subject or theme of their topics.

The competent professional speaker will not only decline to talk on a subject that is not within his area of competence, but will usually suggest another speaker who, in his professional opinion, is best qualified to do the job. As mentioned earlier, do not hesitate to ask a professional speaker for recommendations about other speakers for different spots on your program. He probably will sweat blood, but end up giving you the benefit of a lot of valuable professional know-how and experience.

Of course, if you are financially able you can always book a celebrity—a prominent person, radio, TV or screen star, ex-government official, etc., etc., etc. Practically all of them book through agencies and vary from moderately to extremely expensive, depending on their prominence and drawing power. In the proper program place they are worth what they cost.

Some celebrities are brilliant speakers, very responsive to an audience; others are neither so brilliant or so responsive. Some merely recite the same ghost-written memorized spiel to all audiences, on all occasions. Some are extroverts, some are timid-souls. For example, I have seen a man-in-the-news, apparently an urbane prototype, who could not face an audience without getting as nervous as a fat nudist, with hiccoughs, trying to climb thru a five-strand barbed-wire fence.

However, when you hire a celebrity, radio, TV screen star, etc., you are not primarily buying speaking ability. If they can speak you get a bonus. If they put in an appearance and stand on the podium they delivered most, if not all that you paid for. At a banquet following a two-hour cocktail party and a two-hour dinner, it does not really matter if an alleged speaker can speak.

For the amateur speaker, the part-time speaker, the prominent business man or politician, his commitment to speak at your meeting necessarily has a secondary priority. If a conflict or crisis develops with respect to his principal occupation, he may have to cancel his commitment to your meeting. You should be prepared for this contingency.

Of course if you want an effective speaker attuned to your meeting whose primary business is to deliver the message and produce desired results, but whose name is not necessarily a household word, you are talking about a professional business speaker. Of necessity, the professional speaker has a vested personal interest in the success of your meeting; because his business success depends on making your meeting successful.

> Most business speakers are obtained by clients who contact them directly after getting their name from another speaker or from some of the directories mentioned earlier in this chapter (see page 109). However, some business speakers are booked through agents while others may be booked either way. If a speaker books exclusively through an agent he will refer you to his agent when you contact him. Most business speakers who book by direct contact do so because they desire a personal exchange of ideas and a discussion about the meeting with the executives who are running the meeting.

Although a speaker may not have the exact time and date you want available, *no speaker ever has all dates taken.* He might be booked for Tuesday a year from now and even Tuesday two years from now and still be available every Tuesday next month. Sometimes, you or the speaker can reschedule either your date, day or time to great mutual advantage.

INFORMATION OR ENTERTAINMENT?

Progress in every field of human endeavor depends on the sustained effective exchange of ideas. One of the most effective ways of triggering the creative thinking that produces profitable ideas is to have a thought-provoking, mind-stretching meeting. Yet every organization, industry and profession having a meeting runs the risk of becoming mentally inbred through the process of intellectual incest, by having the same people talking to each other, exchanging the same ideas at meeting after meeting. As a result meetings often create a cross-sterilization of cliches rather than a cross-fertilization of creative, profitable ideas.

> Recently, at dinner following a business meeting, several executives were entertaining their wives with comments about the entertaining speaker who had keynoted their business meeting. Unfortunately one of the wives, suffering from congenital common sense, interrupted her husband to say "Yes, but what did the speaker say?" There were a few feeble attempts to answer this blunt question. Some recalled flip comments, jokes, humorous stories, etc., but no one could answer her question.

Unless the purpose of your meeting is to kill time, or be 100 percent recreational, each speaker should not only be informative, entertaining and socially acceptable, but he should have something worthwhile to say and be able to say it in a way that will not let it be forgotten. That's what profitable meetings are all about.

Good programming is greatly affected by the batting order of speakers and the appetizing variations of the mental menu on your program. Obviously there is little point in having a dynamic speaker hit a mental home run before the bases are loaded. Close each session with a dynamic speaker, and never have a routine paper reader follow an articulate thought-provoking speaker. That's like drinking champagne, then having stagnant water for a chaser.

Similarly, don't permit a speaker to use poor visuals such as slides of typewritten pages, too small to be seen by the audience.

Good programming can be tremendously improved by variety such as using both live speakers and sound-color professionally produced motion pictures that complement each other and provide a change of pace.

Every message delivered at your meeting should be pertinent to your total program. Nothing should be extraneous to your objective. The most effective humor is that which illustrates a point, and even the recreation, such as golf tournaments, can be made pertinent by relevant slogans, such as "The Swinging Seventies Salesman's Sweepstakes."

ESTIMATING COSTS

What do speakers cost? If they are poor speakers they can cost you a fortune by making all or part of your meeting ineffective. A relatively small meeting of 200 people with average earnings of $10,000 to $20,000 per year, has an approximate minimum cost of $1,500 per meeting hour. If a speaker wastes the time of your audience for one hour, he will cost $1,500 even if you got him free. To have a profitable meeting every speaker on your program must be worth more than the time he takes to deliver his message.

Some of the people who do business with you, or who want to do business with you, may provide a speaker from their own organization. If you are lucky, they may pick up the tab and provide you with an outstanding professional speaker. If they provide a speaker from their own organization there is a better-than-average chance that he will be a "paper reader," rendering a talk prepared by someone in his company's advertising department.

However, a few organizations do have excellent speakers associated with them on a retainer basis, which they may provide for your meeting. Increasingly, progressive organizations which have an interest in improving their public relations, or promoting business with your organization, will pick up the tab and provide you with an outstanding professional speaker. From their standpoint, this is frequently a more profitable promotion than providing a hospitality room that will be frequented and forgotten by semi-sober strangers.

Part-time speakers and semi-professional speakers usually have charges ranging from $100 to $300, plus expenses. Full-time professional speakers charge in a variety of ways. Some have a fee, such as $500 plus expenses, regardless of the size of the audience or the nature of the occasion. Others have a minimum fee, plus expenses, for audiences up to a certain size, such as $400 for an audience up to 300 people, then 50¢ per person for each additional person. On this basis, the fee for an audience of 500 people would be $500 plus expenses. In other words, your cost per person declines as the size of the audience increases.

Some speakers charge on the basis of the length of the type of presentation you want. For example, do you want them to make a single presentation or run an all-day workshop, or make two or three different presentations on the same or different days of their program.

If you are a true-believer in the "American Private Enterprise Profit System" do not ask, or expect, a professional speaker to donate his services to your business or professional meeting, any more than you would expect an accountant or a lawyer to donate his services to your legal or economic problems.

All speakers will quote you a flat fee which will include their fee and all expenses. Most speakers, when operating on a fee-plus-expense basis, will pro-rate travel expenses. If they can effect a savings for you by combining travel to two or more engagements, this can result in a substantial saving to you. However, if you elect to pay a flat fee (which includes estimated expenses), you pay that amount regardless of whether travel can be combined. The amount of a flat fee is based on the speaker's normal fee plus his guess of what travel cost will be.

If you are not planning on using all amateur cooks to feed the body, and all amateur bartenders to feed the spirit, why depend on using all amateur speakers to motivate the mind and feed the brain? The human mind is the most sophisticated of all computers. Like all other types of computers, the input and output are irrevocably inter-related. The better your speakers, the better your meeting—it's up to you.

The economics of business meetings are simple—*the only kind of speakers you can afford are effective speakers, just as the only kinds of meetings you can afford are effective meetings.* By using a combination of applied intelligence, industry, initiative, and know-how, a program chairman cannot only get good speakers he can get the cream of the crop. And a productive profitable meeting becomes the inevitable result.

TIMETABLING A PROGRAM

Most programs run behind time almost entirely because of unrealistic planning. Inevitably they will run late because they do not allow for the interim time between events. For example, every year thousands of banquet programs show—

> Cocktails 6 to 7 P.M.
> Dinner 7 to 8 P.M.

The place where the cocktail party is held and where the dinner is going to be served may involve a five minute walk or even waiting for and taking elevators to a different floor. It is obviously impossible for people to simultaneously finish their drink, lay down a cocktail glass in one room, and pick up a fork and start eating their appetizer in another room, even when the rooms are adjoining. Obviously there is going to be time in transit. In addition, while in transit, most of the audience will take a detour to the rest rooms. Realistic planning relies on these assumptions. No matter what was shown on the printed program realistic planning would be based on facts like this—

> Cocktails 6 to 7
> Dinner 7:30 to 8:30 (If you are lucky)

A realistic planner would figure on another half-hour lost due to clearing tables, visits to the rest rooms, etc. etc. So his after-dinner program would be predicated on a 9 P.M. start. He would base the number of events on the fact that the audience had been sitting for 1½ hours before his program starts.

Every program chairman should have engraved on his brain the old Roman slogan:

NIHIL AUDITUR CAUDE DOLENTE

which, translated, means:

"The head can only absorb what the tail can endure."

Awards, presentations and entertainment should follow the speaker. Musical groups can be scheduled during the dinner, and the head table can be introduced during the inevitable dull interval between the entrée and dessert. Unscheduled speakers should not be tolerated and surprise presentations (which never surprise anyone) should be as carefully pre-planned and timed as an extemporaneous remark by Churchill or Roosevelt.

Unrealistic planning is always detrimental to the program. No matter how optimistically the program is printed it will inevitably proceed on a realistic basis. Nothing is gained by starting on time if the starting time is so unrealistic that the room is almost empty. Giving out awards, plaques, introducing the head table, will always take longer than it was assumed they would take.

Whenever you see one of these so-called professional working timetables scheduled to the exact minute such as:

9:01—Salute to flag
9:03—Invocation
9:05—Introduction of presiding officer
9:08—Presiding officer introduces Governor
9:19—Governor concludes
9:20—Presiding officer thanks Governor
9:22—Presiding officer introduces keynote speaker

You can depend on it, that meeting will be thoroughly fouled up.

During the morning business session three scheduled twenty-minute speakers will take up more than one hour. Obviously it will take a couple of minutes to introduce each one and each speaker cannot be introduced until a brief interval after the other speaker finishes. Whether it is planned that way or not, three twenty-minute speakers will use up 90 minutes of program time.

Realistic planning allows leeway for slippage. It is figured to approximately the nearest 5 or 10 minute interval, and it allows for half-hour coffee and/or kidney breaks. That way, if the program starts getting behind, you can reduce a coffee break to 20 minutes and get back on schedule. All good programming should have built into it a "catch-up time," a coffee break or luncheon break that can easily be shortened. Unfortunately, most allowed times for breaks and meals are so unrealistic that it is inevitable that the program will get further behind time. In addition to unrealistic timing, there is always going to be some speaker who goes overtime. Paper-readers in particular fail to allow for the fact that it takes much longer to read a paper aloud over a microphone to an audience than it took either to read it silently, or to read it to an audience of one or two people. If the acoustics of the room tend to echo, everyone has to slow down, and it takes longer.

No one ever got disturbed about a speaker or program that finished on time or even slightly ahead of time.

CHECKLIST OF MEETING BOOBY-TRAPS

During the next year I will participate in more than 100 sales, business, professional, and community meetings. At almost all of these meetings something will go wrong. There will be some kind of a foul up. It may be merely annoying or it may be disastrous, but seldom, if ever, will it be anything new, or something that could not have been easily prevented. These are some of the things that repeatedly go wrong at meetings.

1. The meeting rooms will become too warm, because they were not pre-cooled before the audience filled the room. If the room is comfortable when empty it will inevitably become too warm when you fill it with people.

2. Either the microphones won't work, or will work poorly.

3. The sound-speakers around the room will not be balanced; as a result even if the microphone works the sound will be bad, blasting the people in one part of the room and inaudible to those sitting in a different part of the room.

4. There will be one or more presiding chairmen who will whisper vaguely in the general direction of the microphone then claim it isn't working.

5. The program will get hopelessly behind time because of:
   (a) unrealistic timing.
   (b) speakers who run overtime because they pay no attention to the time allotted them.
   (c) a chairman who, at the conclusion of each talk, keeps asking for questions even though the meeting is already an hour behind schedule.

6. The hotel loudspeaker will blast into the meeting room with music or an announcement that the airport limousine is now leaving.

7. One or more nonprofessional speakers *won't show up.* Worse than that, some will send substitutes to read their paper. The substitute will start by telling the audience he doesn't know anything about the subject and has not had a chance to read the paper previous to the meeting.

8. *A luncheon or dinner will be ruined by a cocktail party* that went much too long.

9. The business or banquet *program will be hopelessly overloaded.*

10. The banquet will come to a tail-wearying halt while they *give out endless golf awards* to each and every person who even went near the golf course.

11. Even though the program was originally overloaded and scheduled too tightly, there will be a couple of *unscheduled presentations* of awards with appropriate speeches by the donor and the recipient—plus time out for photographs.

12. *The size of the meeting rooms will be utterly unrelated* to the size of the audience, such as 150 people in a room that holds 1500. Few things contribute as much to the success of a meeting as a room that is the right size and slightly on the cool side.

13. At 11:30 AM on the morning of the last day, after every-

one has packed his bags, confirmed his return flight and checked out, *the chairman will announce that the check-out time has been extended.*

14. The meeting rooms will be changed after the program has been printed. As a result *most of the time at the meeting will be taken up with incessant announcements that the session scheduled for the Rose Room will be held in the Poison Ivy Room,* while the meeting scheduled for the Robert E. Lee room, will now be held in the General Sherman Room, etc., etc. When this announcement has been completed, someone will ask the chairman to repeat it.

15. *There is always a meeting manager so naive* that he really believed that partition rooms sub-divided by accordian type partitions can be made sound proof. As a result, the banquet speaker may have the not so subtle accompaniment of a teenage bongo band or the audience may hear two or three speakers simultaneously.

16. Then we have the meticulous "i"-dotting, "t"-crossing program chairman who sent the hotel a comprehensive letter with attachments detailing step-by-step instructions about every phase of the convention, *nine months ago.* Since then, he has had no contact with the hotel and sees no need to follow-up since he has already given them all the information they need. Of course, during the intervening nine months the hotel had two changes in management and the man who coordinated the original arrangements is no longer with that hotel. When he left, he took the instruction letter with him.

17. At working business meetings, where sessions go on all day, they will serve a heavy full meal at lunch plus cocktails and then wonder why the afternoon sessions are dull. It would be much simpler and cheaper to serve the audience a sleeping pill.

18. The program chairman will fail to double check the arrangements and then let the meeting-place management make all the last-minute decisions about room lay-out, chair set-ups, etc. Since they have no concept of his priorities of importance, they cannot do the job.

Ghost-writing For the Boss

Sooner or later in the life of every upward-bound junior executive will come the day when he is directed to write a speech for the "Big Boss." Do it well—make the boss look his best—and it will be an important step in your own career. So here are a few tips about ghost-writing.

If at all possible, get the big boss himself to personally discuss his ideas with you and give you some idea of his message and the approach he wishes to take.

If you are lucky, you may get the word from him. Unfortunately you are far more likely to get this information second- or third-hand from a staff member. While the content of this information may be accurate, it will not give you a clue to the nuances of the viewpoint and personality of the boss.

No matter how you get the information, follow the procedures outlined in this book.

Be sure you put the talk into spoken English that will sound like spoken English even if the boss reads the talk. Use short sentences, short words, his vocabulary and his style. In other words, the talk should be tailored to his personality. Like a tailor making a suit, a ghost-writer tailors the material to fit the wearer, not to fit himself.

The better the ghost-writer and his principal understand each other, the more effective they become as a team. When the speaker and his ghost-writer remain strangers, the resulting talk will sound like a ventriloquist's dummy being operated by an inexperienced stranger.

The ghost-writer should record all drafts on tape so that his principal (and his staff) will base their ideas and suggestions on listening to spoken English. If you provide typed drafts, the comments will be based on the reactions *of a reader* instead of a listener. If this happens, much of the value of the suggestions will be lost since the talk will evolve into good reading material instead of spoken English.

If the boss is going to read your written talk, there is a definite typing technique that will make it much easier to read.

Normally, when material is to be read, such as a letter or book, it is customary to indent the first word of each paragraph, as was done in this paragraph.

For effective reading, the process should be reversed and the first word should be projected out and the remainder of the paragraph indented as shown below:

IF WE CAN STAND UP TO HIM, ALL EUROPE MAY BE

FREED AND THE LIFE OF THE WORLD MAY MOVE

FORWARD INTO BROAD SUNLIT UPLAND; BUT IF

WE FAIL THE WHOLE WORLD, INCLUDING THE

UNITED STATES AND ALL THAT WE HAVE KNOWN

AND CARED FOR, WILL SINK INTO THE ABYSS

OF A NEW DARK AGE MADE MORE SINISTER AND

PERHAPS MORE PROLONGED BY THE LIGHTS OF

A PERVERTED SCIENCE.

LET US THEREFORE BRACE OURSELVES TO OUR DUTY AND

SO BEAR OURSELVES THAT IF THE BRITISH

COMMONWEALTH AND EMPIRE LAST FOR A THOUSAND

YEARS, MEN WILL STILL SAY "THIS WAS THEIR

FINEST HOUR."

This makes it much easier for the reader to look up, glance around at the audience, and easily find the first word of the next paragraph when he returns his eyes to the text.

Obviously the talk should be typed double-spaced on a speech typewriter, preferably black type on yellow paper for maximum easy visibility. If a speech typewriter is not available, then it should be typed all capitals. Extreme visability is an absolute must for *effective reading.*

If at all possible every page should end with a completed paragraph, but in no case should part of a sentence dangle over to the next page. Since a reader must pause to turn a page, this pause automatically conveys the impression of a period and the dangling words on the next page create confusion in the minds of his listeners.

If by ending each page with a completed sentence the bottom line ends too high up on the page, it is obvious that the sentences are in written English and too long for effective listening by an audience. In other words these long sentences are in good written English which always makes for poor listening.

There is a technique of preparing a talk so that part of it can be delivered from notes while other parts involving classified, critical or vital exact information can be accurately read. If you elect to use this technique, you alternate one-line notes with complete paragraphs like this:

HISTORY--company--industry

GROWTH--new plans--new products

THE CURRENT UP-TURN OF BUSINESS IS GOING TO CAUSE

    REORGANIZATION AND EXPANSIONS AS FOLLOWS: ALL

    AUTOMOTIVE PARTS MANUFACTURING WILL BE

    CONCENTRATED IN THE NEW DETROIT PLANT.

    AGRICULTURAL EQUIPMENT WILL BE CONCENTRATED IN

    OUR PLANT AT SPRINGFIELD. THE FOLLOWING PLANTS

    WILL BE EXPANDED: SCRANTON, ROANOKE AND

    POUGHKEEPSIE.

IMPACT--suppliers--community

LEAD TIMES

CONCLUSION

Speakers' Basic Information Check List

To avoid embarrassing misunderstandings, to make a more effective presentation, and above all to make an intelligent decision, executives should use a check list to be sure that they have all pertinent information relative to a speaking inquiry.

On page 127 is a practical basic information check list. All items on this list have proven helpful, sometimes vital— none are irrelevant.

Lines 1-2-3-4-5

Contact day of inquiry
Day, date, time, place, purpose, etc.

Groups unexpectedly have changes in committees, program chairman, etc.—People get ill, are sent abroad, change jobs, riots occur. In an emergency, it is very important that you be able to readily and clearly identify your original contact and the facts that he supplied to you.

Lines 6-7-8

Audience background information

This information will provide a profile of the audience. It is pertinent to your decision. If you accept, it will enable you to better attune your remarks to the specific audience. It also may make it clear that this is not the right audience for you and provide the basis for a constructive recommendation.

Lines 9-10-11-12-13-14

Contact name, title, address, phone, etc.

This is the pertinent information about your *working* contact, the person with whom you will coordinate all details of your presentation. Frequently this liaison will be a different individual than the person who originally contacted you. It is most important that you and he be able to contact each other readily. Since business and personal emergencies do not always occur during business hours, it is very important that you have each other's home phone numbers if a crisis arises.

Lines 15-16-17-18
Subject—Time allowed—total program— other speakers—etc.

This is the information you need to decide if participation in this program is to the advantage of your organization. Is the subject in your baliwick? Is the time allowed adequate to treat the subject so as to project a favorable image of your organization and yourself (remember, since unrealistic planning makes most programs run late you will probably get less, not more time.) Are the purposes of the meeting, the general program and the other speakers compatible with the interest and image of your organization?

Lines 19-20-21
News Media, props, financial arrangements

These are the nuts and bolts of effective appearances. If there is going to be news media publicity either before, during, or after the meeting, you should know about it so that photos, press digests, etc. can be made available. Also, if you need an overhead slide projector, blackboard or other props, these details should be worked out in advance.

Similarly, financial arrangements about who pays for what should be mutually understood in advance. Were you offered an opportunity to participate at your expense or did they invite you at their expense?

Line 22
Remarks

This is the catch-all to include the unusual or any nuances you should know about.

Line 23
Decision

This is for your own information and future reference.

SPEAKERS' BASIC INFORMATION CHECK LIST

1. *Original contact*   Date _____

   Name _____Title _____Organization _____

   Address _____Phone _____

   How contacted _____Phone _____Letter _____

2. *Date of Event:*   Year   Month   Day   Date   Time

3. City _____State _____

4. Place _____

5. Purpose of meeting _____

6. *Audience*   Size _____

7.   Men _____Women _____Children _____

8.   Composition: _____

9. My working contact _____

10.   Title _____

11.   Organization _____

12.   Address _____

13.   City _____State _____Zip _____

14.   Phone—Office *area code*_____*Number*_____*Ext.*_____

        Home *area code*_____*Number*_____

15. Subject of Talk _____

16. Time allowed _____

17. Outline of program _____

18. Other speakers who have accepted:

    _____

    _____

    _____

19. *News Media*   *Digests*   *Photos*

20. Props _____

21. Financial Arrangements_____Expenses_____Honorarium_____

22. Remarks _____

23. Decision _____

The Intelligent Salesman's Guide
to Group Soft-selling

The salesman who can only talk to one or two people at a time, and who has not yet learned to talk to a group, is throwing away his opportunity to be a champion.

Most people are reluctant to make an appointment with a wide variety of salesmen including securities salesmen and particularly the salesman who wants to sell more insurance. As a result most insurance salesmen have to invest a lot of time in getting an appointment with a single prospect, before they even get an opportunity to make a sale.

> A few years ago I attended a luncheon and listened to an insurance salesman give an informative and highly entertaining talk on the history of the insurance industry. He fascinated and intrigued us with entertaining historical stories about the early days when people used to try to take out insurance on dying strangers. He regaled us with colorful frauds that had been tried. He dramatized the evolution and progress of his industry from fly-by-night, unregulated companies to the standards of today's ethical companies.

> With wit and wisdom he informed us of the advantages and disadvantages of various types of insurance. While he pleasantly displayed a thorough knowledge of his business, he avoided all the usually befuddling terminology and made no apparent sales talk. Within forty minutes most of us became more intelligently informed about insurance and had a better appreciation of its part in our plans than we previously obtained from all the insurance salesmen we had talked to in a lifetime.

> The result was that many of us were calling him for appointments to have him look over and evaluate our insurance programs. One forty minute talk eliminated his need to search for prospects one at a time. He literally obtained prospects wholesale. Because his talk was good, he never lacked for invitations to speak. Chairmen sought him because his previous audiences praised his performance on the platform.

In view of the payoff, you would think that most salesmen would invest time in learning to speak to groups. The unfortunate fact is that many salesmen cannot give an interesting talk to a group about the product on which they and their families depend for economic survival.

DO YOU KNOW YOUR BUSINESS?

No matter what business you are in, or no matter what product you sell, if you like your work you can make that occupation the subject of an interesting, informative and entertaining talk.

Start by reading up on the history of your business or profession. Where, when and how did it get started? Even the origin of accounting and bookkeeping can be made exciting. Did you ever try bookkeeping or accounting with Roman numerals? The history of engineering is a romance between man and his dreams from flying carpet to the latest jet. Do you know the origin of the term civil engineer? Almost every business, industry, and profession has had its share of fascinating characters, colorful pioneers that range from dull saints to dynamic s-o-b's. (See Appendix V, Page 134.)

After you look up the history of your industry or profession, then proceed to find where it fits in today's world. Now that you know where the industry has been, start taking some guesses at where it is going.

> Before talking to any group made up largely of one industry or profession, I always try to acquire some appreciation of their contribution to civilization by reading the history of that field of activity. As a result, when I am met at the airport by someone from that group, I usually have a number of unanswered questions about his industry, company or profession. Time and again, I am amazed to find that this person, who has been identified with that activity most of his working life, knows little or nothing about it, except in terms of his department and his personal day-to-day activity. Like a ship at sea without a compass he does not know whether he or his organization is coming or going. All he knows is that they are on their way.

THE CONSUMER APPROACH

Every community in America has hundreds of meetings or even thousands of meetings every year. There are groups that meet weekly, monthly or quarterly. There are business, professional, community, church, company, industry, trade, PTA's, men's groups, women's groups, civic groups, community groups, etc. etc. Americans are the "meeting-ist" people on earth.

All of these "little or no budget groups" have programs and harried program chairmen (or chairladies) all trying desperately to meet an increasingly insatiable demand for alleged speakers who have something interesting to say to their group.

Although these groups vary widely in major goals, their occupations, interests, ages, economic and educational levels, etc. etc. All their members have one thing in common:

> *Every member of every group is a consumer, every member of every audience either makes or influences the purchasing decision of an entire family.*

Every member of every one of these audiences intends to continue enjoying, or improve, the standard of living to which he or she is currently accustomed. The people who attend meetings are seldom at the lower economic levels. They have purchasing power. No matter how well they are living now, they plan to improve it. Young married couples don't start out where their parents did. They use their parents' standard of living as a launching pad. Parents no longer try to keep up with the Jones's. Frequently they are trying to keep up with their married children's constantly improving standard. Every succeeding generation raises not only the standard of material comforts, but also cultural enjoyments. In many homes good music, like running water, is available 24 hours a day.

Because they are culturally programmed for continuous improvement, the American consumer constantly up-dates his standard of living by buying automobiles, books, refrigerators, radios, hi-fi's, TV, better food, clothing, insurance, leisure and lawn equipment, etc., etc., etc. The American consumer does not have a choice of "to buy" or "not to buy." Most Americans are compulsive consumers. Their continuous decision is what to buy next, when to buy it, where to buy it, and how to buy it.

Every member of every audience is a consumer craving more knowledge about the products and services *he will inevitably buy.* He wants to know the advantages and disadvantages of the infinite variety of choices that confront and confuse him every time he makes a purchase.

Because all these meetings desire speakers, and because all the members of the audience crave more and more knowledge about available products and services, there is a continuous demand for business and professional men who have a thorough knowledge of the industry, their product or service *and who are also effective speakers.* These are men who can interestingly and intelligently discuss their business, from the consumers' viewpoint (while scrupulously avoiding a sales approach). They will never lack for speaking engagements, customers or clients. All consumers are searching for business and professional men who not only know their own business but who also demonstrate they have an understanding and appreciation of the problems, interest and needs of the consumer. We are all impressed by the business or professional man who demonstrates *the willingness to render a service, to meet a need without any assurance of immediate personal gain.*

The United States is probably the only country in the world where people work harder searching for competent salesmen than salesmen work seeking customers.

We all envy the fellow who, when he needs something, can pick up the phone and confidently start buying it because he is lucky enough to know and have justifiable confidence in a truly professional, competent salesman. He not only has confidence that the salesman knows his business, but also has confidence in the fact that the salesman knows his needs and has the integrity to relate the product or service to those needs at a fair price. This way both the buyer and the seller profit by the transaction. The professional salesman sells satisfaction while the order-taker merely distributes products.

The salesman who can interestingly, and intelligently, inform (rather than attempt to sell an audience) will have prospects knocking at his door, or ringing his phone. He can spend his time profitably servicing customers, not unprofitably hunting prospects.

Under these circumstances you would think most salesmen would learn how to be effective speakers. Unfortunately, this is not the case. As a program chairman you would be hard put to find an interesting and effective speaker on such "in-demand" subjects as:

> Buying your next home
> Keeping your insurance program current
> How to buy a "second" car
> When, where and how to make a will
> To buy or to rent—that's the question
> What your bank can do for you
> How to recognize quality in . . . . ?

There are probably more unskilled salesmen than unskilled laborers in the United States. The skilled salesman knows that before he can sell a product or service he must first create confidence by psychologically selling himself. The salesman who is an effective public speaker can sell himself wholesale when he addresses an audience. Later, when individual members of that audience contact him, all he then has to do is render a service or sell a product.

Recently, in a major metropolitan area, they had a banquet and presented a "plaque" to the alleged "Salesman of the Year." Unfortunately, he attempted to give a so-called acceptance speech. It was so long and so bad that some members of the organization tried to start a movement to recall the award. They ended up firing the committee that selected him for the recipient of "The Salesman of the Year" award.

FINDING YOUR AUDIENCE

The competent man who has a product to sell or a service to offer should *first* become an effective speaker, then make himself available to appropriate audiences to make a worthwhile presentation at their meeting. To get the first couple of audiences may take some effort. After that, if he makes an effective, competent presentation, using a consumer rather than a sales approach, the demand for his services as a speaker will snowball.

To get that first couple of public appearances, he may want to write or phone some program chairman or get one of the group's members to bring his availability to the attention of the organization.

Almost every area has groups such as Rotary, Kiwanis, Lions, Exchange Club. Then there are industry, business and professional clubs, church clubs, fraternal and veterans organizations, business and professional women, youth groups, middle age groups, senior citizens groups, etc. Since the profile of each group is different, some of these groups will be exceptionally appropriate for different subjects. You might write the chairman a letter on your letterhead along these lines:

> Dear Mr. _____:
>
>   As the program chairman of _____ you are undoubtedly looking for program material that will be interesting, timely and helpful to your members. Because I think interesting meetings are an important part of our community life, I would like to assist you by providing part of your program.
>
>   Obviously every member of your organization is a "consumer"—sooner or later he is going to have to make a purchasing decision about a product or service on which his knowledge is necessarily limited. I would like to attend one of your meetings and put on a brief, interesting and informative program on
>
> _____
> _____
>
> Because this subject is my business I am knowledgeable about it. However, I will not make a sales talk at your meeting. My approach will be from the consumer's viewpoint. I want to make your members better informed consumers. From this program they will gain a better knowledge of the advantages and disadvantages of the choices available to them. Also, they will become more aware of personal and family factors they should carefully consider in making this type of decision.
>
>   In summary my program will not be sales oriented—it will be brief, interesting and informative.
>
>   Please give me a call so I can learn more about your organization and their interests. I am looking forward to hearing from you.
>
>   Sincerely,

Standard References

Everyone who gives talks or prepares talks and press digests for news media should have readily available such standard references as:

(1) A good dictionary; Roget's Thesaurus
(2) Bartlett's Quotations
(3) A reference on American English Usage such as:
    (a) Fowler's Modern English Usage
    (b) A dictionary of American-English Usage by Margaret Nicholson (available in paperback—A Signet Book published by New American Library.)
(4) World Almanac or Reader's Digest Almanac
(5) "Speakers Encyclopedia of Stories, Quotations and Anecdotes" by Jacob M. Braude (Prentice-Hall)
(6) "The Speaker's Special Occasion Book" by Maxwell Droke (Grossett and Dunlap) This is a collection of material related to festivals, holidays and seasons of the year.

Language—Verbal—Non Verbal Communication

The person who becomes intrigued with the miracle of language, including its nuances and subtleties, will discover a wealth of material in such paperbacks as:

The Miracle of Language by Charlton Laird (A Premier Book - Fawcett World Library)

Language for Everybody by Mario Pei (Pocket Books, Inc.)

The Treasure of Our Tongue by Lincoln Barnett (Mentor Books)

Watch Your Language by Theodore M. Bernstein (Pocket Books Inc.)

The Silent Language by Edward T. Hall (Fawcett Premier Paperback)

Body Language by Julius Fast (Pocket Books, Inc.)

For references relating to *Private Enterprise, Profit and Loss System,* see:

The Mainspring of Human Progress by Henry Grady Weaver (Foundation for Economic Education, Irvington on Hudson, New York)

Capitalism—The Unknown Ideal by Ayn Rand (A Signet Book - The New American Library 1967)

The Communist Manifesto by Karl Marx and Friedrick Engles (Washington Square Press, N.Y. and numerous other publishers)

The Capitalist Manifesto by Louis O. Kelso & Mortimer J. Adler (Random House, N.Y. 1958)

The Forbes Scrapbook of Thoughts on the Business of Life (Forbes Inc. New York 1950)

Why Did They Name It—? by Hannah Campbell (An Ace Star Book (paperbook) 1964)

American Battle for Abundance by Charles Kettering and Allen Orth (General Motors 1947)

My Years with General Motors by Alfred P. Sloan Jr. Macfadden-Bartnell, New York)

My Forty Years with Ford by Charles E. Sorenson (Collier Books, New York)

Prophet of Progress (Selections from the speeches of Charles F. Kettering) Edited by T. A. Boyd (E. P. Dutton and Company, Inc. New York)

For references to *Particular Business and Industry,* see:

Fads and Fallacies in the Name of Science by Martin Gardner (Ballentine Books 1952)

The Shocking History of Advertising by E. S. Turner (Ballentine Books 1953)

The 100 Greatest Advertisements (Who Wrote Them and What They Did) by Julian Lewis Watkins (Dover Publications, 180 Varick St., N.Y.)

Classified Humor (Advertising) by Earle Tempel (Pocket Books, Inc. 1 W-39th St., New York, N.Y. 1970)

Wells Fargo (Transportation of People and Gold) by Edward Hungerford (Bonanza Books - Crown Publishers, 419 Park Avenue, South, New York, New York)

Harvest Triumphant (Farm Machinery) by Merrill Denison (Dodd, Mead & Company, New York)

The World of Mr. Sheraton (Hotel History) by Ernest Henderson (Popular Library, New York)

Five and Ten (Retail Merchandising) (The Fabulous Life of F. W. Woolworth) by John K. Winkler (Bantam Books, Inc.)

The Metropolitan Life (Insurance) by Marquis James (The Viking Press)

The Cord of Steel (Telephone) by Thomas B. Costain (Pocket Books, Inc., New York)

Sixty Years of the Independent Telephone Movement by Francis X. Welch (U.S. Independent Telephone Assoc., Washington, D. C.)

How Much Do You Know About *Glass?* by Harlan Logan (Dodd, Mead, and Company)

The Yankee Peddlers of Early America by J. R. Dolan (Bramhall House, New York)

For reference relating to *Medicine-Drugs-Pharmaceuticals,* see:

The Eternal Search by Richard Mathison (G. P. Putnam's Sons, Madison Avenue, N.Y.)

The Amazing World of Medicine by Helen Wright and Samuel Rapport (Harper and Row, New York)

Devils, Drugs and Doctors by Howard W. Haggard, M.D. (Pocket Books, Inc.)

The Men Who Made Surgery" by Agatha Young (Bartholomew House (Hillman Books) New York)

Fifty Years a Surgeon by Robert T. Morris, M.D. (A Signet Key Book)

The Astonishing History of the Medical Profession by E. S. Turner (Ballentine Books)

New Frontiers in Medicine" by Stanley Englebardt (Pyramid Books)

Magic, Myth and Medicine by D. T. Atkinson, M.D. (A Premier Book, Fawcett Publications)

For reference to *Manufacturing - Machinery,* see:

Machines That Built America by Roger Burlingame (Harcourt, Brace and Company) (Signet Books - New American Library 1955)

The Epic of American Industry by James Blaine Walker (Harper and Brothers)

Fathers of Industry by Leonard M. Fanning (A Macfadden-Bartnell Book)

American Science and Invention (A Pictorial History) by Mitchell Wilson (Simon and Schuster, New York)

Yankee Science in the Making by Dirk J. Struik (Collier Books)

Inventors in Action by James Thomas Flexner (Collier Books)

Scientists Behind the Inventors by Roger Burlingame (Avon Books)

A History of Mechanical Inventions by Abbott Payson Usher (Beacon Press, Beacon Hill, Boston)

March of the Iron Men by Roger Burlingame (Universal Library)

Tinkers and Genius (The story of the Yankee inventors) by Edmund Fuller (Hastings House, New York)

For reference material about *Transportation,* see:

Pictorial History of American Ships (on the High Seas and Inland Waters) by John and Alice Durant (A. S. Barnes and Company, N.Y.)

Wheels Across America by Clarence P. Hornung (A. S. Barnes and Company, New York)

Fares, Please by John Anderson Miller (Dover Publications Inc., New York)

The Wright Brothers by Fred C. Kelly (Ballentine Books, New York)

The American Automobile by John B. Rae (The University of Chicago Press)

The Insolent Chariots by John Keats (J. B. Lippincott) (Crest Books, Fawcett World Library)

The Shape of the Motor Car by Leslie A. Everett (Roy Publishers, New York)

Cities in the Motor Age by Wilfred Owen (The Viking Press, New York)

Boeing 707 by Martin Caidin (Ballentine Books)

Trailer-Travel (Here & Abroad) by Wally Byam (David McKay Company, New York)

For *Early American Living, Craftsmanship and Culture,* see:

Colonial Living

Colonial Craftsman

Frontier Living

Indians

Oars, Sails and Steam

The Young United States

Wheels

Weapons

All of the above are exceptionally interesting, loaded with colorful information, written and illustrated by:

Edwin Tunis (Published by World Publishing Company, N.Y. and Cleveland)

Translating Statistics into Meaningful Illustrations

In order to translate sums of U.S. money into effective pictorial comparisons it is only necessary to know simple arithmetic, and a few facts about the dimensions of U.S. currency.

All U.S. paper currency since July 10, 1929 is of the same size regardless of denomination. A $1 bill, a $1000 bill, or any U.S. paper currency is:

6.14″ inches long
2.61″ inches wide
.0043″ inches thick

A one inch stack of new bills (not compressed) contains 233 bills, a one foot stack would contain 2,796 bills. A stack of bills 12 feet high would contain about 33,500 pieces of currency.

There are approximately 500 pieces of paper currency to a pound.

One million notes would weigh approximately one ton (2,000 pounds) and take up approximately 42 cubic feet of space; for example a space equal to 3 feet $\times$ 7 feet $\times$ 2 feet $=$ 42 cubic feet.

When developing a pictorial example of money remember to specify the denominations of the currency involved. For example:

a ton of $1 bills $=$ $1,000,000 (one million)
a ton of $1,000 bills $=$ $1,000,000,000 (one billion)

One million bills of any U.S. denomination laid end to end would stretch 1,000,000 $\times$ 6.14″ $=$ 6,140,000 inches or approximately 97 miles, the distance between Philadelphia and Baltimore.

Similarly if you stacked one million bills on top of each other, it would work out like this:

1,000,000 $\times$ .0043 $=$ 4,300 inches or 358 feet

358 feet is about the height of a 30-story building

While there is no uniform exact measurement for the height of one story of a modern building, usually it is between 11½ and 12 feet.

Everyone theoretically is in favor of a careful examination of the U.S. annual budget of more than 200 billion dollars. Let's see how long it would take a committee of businessmen to thoroughly examine the budget if we allowed them one hour for each million dollars.

$$\$200,000,000,000 \div 1,000,000 = 200,000 \text{ hours}$$

If they substantiated a million dollars every hour, 24 hours a day, 365 days per year, with no time off for good behavior, it would take more than 22 years! Of course if you wanted to complete the examination in one year with people working normal 40 hour weeks and taking two-week vacations but no holidays it would work out like this

$$40 \text{ hours} \times 50 \text{ weeks} = 2,000 \text{ hours one man per year}$$
$$200,000 \div 2,000 = 100 \text{ full time workers}$$

still allowing only 1 hour for each proposed million dollar expenditure, and no coffee breaks or rest periods.

In United States and England, (but not in Ireland) an acre of ground is 4,840 square yards or 43,560 square feet or 6,272,640 square inches. So if you want to find out how many bills it would take to cover an acre of ground all you have to do is divide the square inches in one acre (6,272,640) by the number of square inches in a paper bill of U.S. money (16.0254″).

$$\frac{6,272,640}{16.0254} = 391,418$$

A billion dollars in one dollar bills would cover an acre 2,555 layers deep. How high?

If you work for the government and can only figure in billions—just remember what you call a billion and what an Englishman calls a billion is quite different. In the U.S. and France, a billion is a thousand million, while in England a billion means a million million.

Related BNA Films
featuring Joe Powell

UNACCUSTOMED AS THEY ARE . . . *An Executive Briefing on Effective Speaking* is an invaluable addition for your film library. In the film, Joe Powell demonstrates how an executive who doesn't do his homework can "bomb" when he presents a talk. With the aid of cartoons, he presents and describes the importance of his ten points to preparing and presenting an effective speech.

Whether he is speaking to his own colleagues at a staff meeting, or addressing an international convention, this "how-to" film will benefit every executive, manager, salesman and professional in your organization.

UNACCUSTOMED AS THEY ARE . . . is available for preview, rental or purchase as follows:

Preview: $15—for executive evaluation only. Prints must be returned within 48 hours of receipt.
Rental: $50 per week
Purchase: $345 each print.

To order, telephone or write to BNA FILMS, 5615 Fishers Lane, Rockville, Maryland 20852 (301) 881-2090.

THE REAL SECURITY has been a "smash hit" in business and industry throughout the Free World. Joe tackles one of the toughest problems facing American management—the fear of change—and offers a new concept of security that can reduce resistance to change and help eliminate "mental retirement".

Purchase: $275 each print   Rental: $45 a week   Preview: $15 (48 hrs)

YOU, YOURSELF, INCORPORATED presents Joe as he motivates people to make the most of their talents. "No matter who your employer is, you are always the sole owner of yourself! You are your own top management!" Blending the serious and the humorous, he demonstrates that the only real development is self-development. "Every motivated man can do more than he thinks he can. Motivated men make progress and profits."

Purchase: $275 each print   Rental: $45 a week   Preview: $15 (48 hrs)

To order, telephone or write to BNA FILMS, 5615 Fishers Lane, Rockville, Maryland 20852 (301) 881-2090.

THE HERITAGE OF THE UNCOMMON MAN—"America was not made great by common men; it was made great by uncommon men. The greatness of America is the right of man to become an uncommon man." In this film Joe Powell again proves his ability to stimulate people to take a bigger look at their potential and opportunities. Aided by a colorful cast of cartoon characters, Joe dramatizes the creative impact of uncommon men—from Colonial pioneers of yesterday to today's pioneers of progress.

This film received the 1967 Freedoms Foundation at Valley Forge Award.

Purchase: $275 each print   Rental: $45 a week   Preview: $15 (48 hrs)

To order, telephone or write to BNA FILMS, 5615 Fishers Lane, Rockville, Maryland 20852 (301) 881-2090.

INDEX